They Call Me Trusty

"The courage and character of Trusty was second to none. He was a dedicated Black firefighter who worked tirelessly over many years to better Black representation in this nation's fire service. This book is a testament to his beliefs and struggles. It also identifies several of the problems he—along with many others—faced in the fire service across this country. I proudly give my support to what has been written."

—**RAYMOND BROOKS**, Retired Fire Chief, Birmingham, Alabama

"There were several individuals and groups who started protesting, talking, having meetings, and using the media to confront race issues, hiring minorities, discrimination, favoritism, and bias in Santa Clara County, California, civil service jobs. The person who stood out the most regarding the fire service was Dudley Bynoe. He was driven with passion, a fierce competitor, and persisted in the face of resistance. His leadership, determination, negotiating skills, and selflessness were the foundation for starting the Santa Clara County Black Firefighters Association. People of color received the benefits of Bynoe's support and sacrifice. He was the main ingredient that desegregated the fire service in Santa Clara County. I became a better person by knowing and working with him."

—**RICHARD P. SANTOS**, Retired Fire Captain, San Jose, California

"I am honored to endorse *They Call Me Trusty* by Dudley Bynoe. I knew Trusty for over forty-five years and worked with him for five years at San Jose Fire Department Station 16. Our time together was one of personal enlightenment and respect for what I witnessed in his life, both within and outside the fire service—a man of great conviction, honor, pride, love, and resiliency. Truly, Trusty Bynoe was a unique spirit who broke down divisive barriers and touched many lives! He became a good friend during our active fire service career and into our retirement years. Our most cherished time was having lunch and playing golf regularly. I considered him a true friend and mentor who would spend hours sharing his 'Bynoeisms' on life. His memoir is a powerful tribute to his convictions, courage, and stories that needed to be told. May he rest in peace and may his memories and warrior spirit be fondly remembered."

—**JERRY FLOYD**, Co-founder, California
Association of Professional Firefighters

"Trusty Bynoe's autobiography is a profound and necessary reflection on courage, conviction, and legacy. His journey during times of civil unrest and institutional resistance to change laid the foundation for young Black firefighters, like myself, to walk with pride and purpose. Trusty's tireless work in the fight for social justice, both within and beyond the fire service, speaks to a life lived in servitude of others and driven by unshakable values. I am deeply grateful for the example he set, the barriers he broke, and the personal mentorship and friendship we've shared. His story is not just history—it's a guidepost for the future."

—**DARIAN WARE**, Firefighter, Presidio of Monterey

"With fires burning inside and outside the Fire Service, Dudley Bynoe demonstrated how he was capable of fighting both. Growing up during a time when the odds were stacked against the Black race, Trusty tells you how he beat the system his way. There is a time when it is necessary to scream at the top of your lungs, and Trusty did this for the benefit of the men and women of San Jose Fire Service and the Fire Service as a whole."

—**TERESA DELOACH REED**, Retired Fire Chief, Oakland Fire Department

They Call Me Trusty

A Black Firefighter's Fight for Social Justice

DUDLEY C. BYNOE

Edited by Linda Turner Bynoe

Foreword by Darrell J. Wesley

Epilogue by Carl Lacey

RESOURCE *Publications* • Eugene, Oregon

Resource Publications
An Imprint of Wipf and Stock Publishers
199 W. 8th Ave., Suite 3
Eugene, OR 97401

www.wipfandstock.com

PAPERBACK ISBN: 978-1-62564-074-1
HARDCOVER ISBN: 978-1-4982-8649-7
EBOOK ISBN: 978-1-7252-4867-0
VERSION NUMBER 07/28/25

Contents

Contents

Audience and Adult Content

THIS BOOK USES STRONG language in several chapters. This may be of concern for some children.

Foreword

By Darrell J. Wesley

There are those in this life who possess something special, an essence that rises above the fray of ordinary existence. They possess what the ancient Greeks call *daimon*, a spiritual something, as it were, a guide that brings out the best in all of us—like that philosophical master Socrates, whose daimon was "improving the souls" of fellow Athenians. If, in our short lives, we enjoy the great fortune of encountering such a griot, that encounter makes all the difference in the world. It was my pleasure to enjoy such an encounter in real time, and it is your pleasure, as a reader, to learn of him through this written account. This memoir, *They Call Me Trusty*, is a heartfelt manifesto of hope, recounting the storied existence of an extraordinary person I saw as a spiritual guide. Those fortunate enough to learn from him are indeed the benefactors of one of life's greatest gifts. We know him by his nickname, Trusty, a name bequeathed to Dudley Bynoe at an early age by his elementary school classmates. Chapter 1 of this masterpiece recounts how his middle school teacher deliberately selected him as the class trustee because of his honesty and trustworthiness. And from that time onward, the nickname Trusty manifested a life of its own. How fitting and apropos. Trusty never wavered in his commitment to the community he lived in and served. In a word, it was his "daimon" to be like his kindred spirit, Socrates. Like his kindred spirit, Trusty was a gadfly to the perpetrators of injustice and a spokesperson for the many muted voices of those who lived on the margins. He knew his calling early on. The first part of this memoir states it clearly: "Throughout my life, even as a child growing up in New York, I have felt a deep responsibility to speak out for justice and to advocate for the voiceless." Those of us who knew him well acknowledge, without hesitation, our trust in his allegiance to the amelioration of injustice and his selfless sacrifice to those in need of assistance, encouragement, and affirmation.

I know firsthand that the nickname Trusty is more than just an arbitrary notion or an accidental epitaph. He came looking for me, if we let him tell the story of our fortuitous encounter. He and his wife, Dr. Linda Bynoe, attended a recognition ceremony at the First Baptist Church of Pacific Grove, California. This annual celebration recognized citizens of the Monterey Peninsula who had recently graduated from schools of every level of education. It was my honor to give the keynote address that day, and though we did not make each other's acquaintance that day, his testimony is that he came looking for me.

Moreover, to my good fortune, he happened upon one of the newer St. James Christian Methodist Episcopal Church members who touted the virtues of his new church home. After mentioning my name as his pastor, Trusty, like a pilgrim with a purpose, says, "I have been looking for that dude." The following Sunday, Trusty, Dr. Linda Bynoe, and their daughters, Traci and Nicola, came through the doors of this little church. I noticed them right away. However, no one could miss them. Six-foot-something Trusty, Dr. Linda Bynoe, with elegance and grace, and two beautiful daughters arrested everyone's attention. I was eager to meet them. As was my routine in those days, immediately following the benediction, I hurried to the back of the church to greet people as they left the sanctuary. To my good fortune, Trusty and his family waited till after I greeted everyone and shared with me the intentionality of their visit. His side of the story is that after hearing me speak at the First Baptist Church of Pacific Grove, he wanted to sit under my teaching as his pastor. My side of the story is that after much searching, my teacher, my spiritual guide, found me. That was 2006, nearly two years after my father, Edward Charles Wesley, died of lung cancer.

Moreover, from that day onward, Trusty Bynoe was a surrogate father. The life lessons I received from him transcended my previous education, which included a master's at Yale and a PhD from Claremont Graduate University. He taught me the importance of selfless service to the community and how to believe in myself, my values, and my self-worth.

His life was my textbook. I listened to the details of a narrative that produced a prophet of social justice. To be sure, Trusty was a prophet following the likeness of Old Testament truth tellers like Amos and Micah. In fact, as the eulogist for his memorial service in January 2023, I titled the message, "The Celebration of an Unofficial Prophet." Trusty's legacy was similar to that of the prophet Amos of Tekoa, who often spoke truth to power with surgical polemics against the imperialist powers of his day. In a scathing critique of the imperialist prophetic Amaziah, Amos announces, "I was neither a prophet nor the son of a prophet" (Amos 7:14 NIV). In other words, Amos claims he did not get an ordination for professional prophecy. However, his prophetic witness lamented how imperialist and religious institutions ignored justice and the plight of the oppressed. Trusty represented that same prophetic tradition. Though not an official preacher, he still, with unparalleled conviction, criticized those who used their power and privilege to perpetuate oppression. Please do not take my word for it. Read this memoir and see for yourself. In the first chapter, Trusty lists a chorus of heroes and sheroes whose voices sang loud amid the noise of racism, sexism, disenfranchisement, injustice, and marginalization. Trusty lists the voices that will never fade from our collective consciousness. Trusty carefully shows their impact on the world, whether in sports, the military, politics, music, literature, or business. Jack Johnson, Joe Louis, and Jackie Robinson in sports; A. J. Smitherman and O. W. Gurley in business; and Lorraine Hansberry, Marcus Garvey, and Thurgood Marshall in arts and politics are some of the names on this list. And with an unassuming yet humble posture, our author makes a modest disclaimer. He humbly states, "I do not compare my humble efforts and modest contributions to social justice with the monumental achievements of the heroes and sheroes." However, for the record, I add one last disagreement to the many debates and the intellectual sparring throughout our extraordinary relationship. Like the consequential list of the names above, Dudley "Trusty" Bynoe deserves inclusion in this chorus of consequential voices.

He came from humble beginnings as the third child of six to Dudley, a Barbados immigrant, and Ruby, a second-generation American of Barbados descent. His mother, Ruby, worked for the janitorial department at New York University (NYU), and Dudley Sr. worked as a bookkeeper for several small businesses. Trusty's education and social justice training did not occur at some higher learning institution. Instead, as he recounts in this memoir, his education commences with the pedagogical genius of one he affectionately calls Granny. With her Bajan accent, Granny taught him about life, accountability to one's community, and the virtue and value of hard work. Like any teacher, Granny discerned Trusty's gift of innovation and critical thinking. These gifts and Granny's wisdom paid dividends for the next seventy years of Trusty's life. There will be other teachers along the way. For example, Trusty gained much insight from his Zen Buddhist teacher, Gia-fu Feng, whom he met during a brief separation from his wife. During that separation, Trusty studied Zen Buddhism for eighteen months at a retreat in the Santa Cruz mountains. The commune's founder and guru, Gia-fu Feng, translated the philosophy of Zen Buddhism from Eastern culture to Western culture. Only a quarter of a century old, this time, for Trusty, precipitated growth beyond his years. It was a period of inward reflection that came from meditation, tai chi, and the philosophy of mindfulness. Finally, one cannot underestimate the intellectual and political growth of his lifelong partner and interlocutor, Dr. Linda Bynoe. Herself a force with which to contend, Dr. Bynoe, a social activist, womanist scholar, cultural critic, and professor of liberal studies, deserves credit for shaping Trusty's vision of social justice. She was a partner in the truest sense of the word.

Alas, we come to the subtitle of this memoir, which essentially signals the experiences and challenges of an African American firefighter. He was one of the first, if not *the* first, African American firefighters for the city of San Jose. Anyone who has been the first of anything knows that depiction comes with its challenges. One has a choice to assimilate and acquiesce to the status quo of the context, or one can exemplify courage in the face of mistreatment, marginalization, and pejorative misconceptions about one's race, gender, and sexuality. Trusty chose the latter, even though he faced the risk of professional martyrdom. To this extent, this story is much more than merely elucidating what it is like to be one of the first firefighters in San Jose, California. Rather, I recommend that readers look at the story behind the story. This story behind the story entails themes of courage, speaking truth to power, risk-taking, and accountability. As I noted at the beginning of this foreword, the story behind the story is how one man lives out his "daimon"—that is, how one man lived his life doing what the universe intended for him to do. *They Call Me Trusty* explains why we who believed in him, relied on him, loved him, and celebrated him called him Trusty. Read this story carefully and hang on to every word, every sentence, every paragraph, every page, and every chapter. Do that, and *They Call Me Trusty* will be a resource of hope, inspiration, and empowerment for you, igniting a fire to make a difference in your piece of the world.

Acknowledgments

By Dr. Linda Turner Bynoe

They Call Me Trusty has been a journey of love, resilience, and collaboration. This book began with the many stories Trusty wrote in his journals and on notepads—words filled with his passion, wisdom, and determination. Deciphering his notes often felt like a conversation with him, a journey into his world, where his voice guided me even in his absence. I leaned on the insights of his friends, who helped ensure that the story remained true to his perspective. I am deeply grateful to everyone who encouraged me during the first challenging year, a time filled with grief, uncertainty, and doubt. Even though I faced many challenges, my family and friends encouraged me to write the book.

To my family—Nicola Bynoe, Vine Samuels, Shemane and Russell Steppe, Lacy Atkinson, Rev. Darrell Wesley, Bridget Davis, Carl Lacey, Gail Robinson Pickens, Darian, and Ana Ware—I thank you for your unwavering support, optimism, and love, which sustained me in moments of doubt. I am endlessly appreciative to the firefighters who visited, called, and shared meals with me, offering their steadfast encouragement as I navigated life without Trusty. My sister friends, who reminded me of the power of purpose, were an invaluable source of strength and inspiration.

Special thanks go to Chief Lacy Atkinson, whose insights into Trusty's inner world were instrumental in shaping this story. I am also deeply grateful to Chief Teresa Deloach Reed, whose editorial expertise and understanding of Trusty's storytelling style clarified the technical language and imagery. I would like to express my gratitude to Chief Robert Osby, Chief Raymond Brooks, Roland Hooks, Doug Potter, Richard Santos, Dave Washington, and Marvin Coffee. Your statements and research significantly contributed to shaping the story. I would also like to acknowledge Marvin, who sadly passed away in February 2023. He generously shared his court case files before his death, which was an invaluable gift to this project.

I would also like to acknowledge Rev. Dr. Darrell Wesley for his thoughtful foreword and guidance in navigating the publishing process. To Carl Lacey, my family for over forty years, thank you for your poignant epilogue and your endless patience in helping me with the technical aspects of the publishing requests. Whenever I sought help, these individuals were there, ready to answer questions, share memories, and support my efforts.

Because of Trusty's vivid imagery and the intimacy captured in his notes, I found inspiration in every word he left behind. This book demanded courage, and I owe its completion to the unwavering love, wisdom, and encouragement of so many. To all who have supported me in bringing Trusty's story to life, I offer my deepest gratitude. Without you, *They Call Me Trusty* would not have been possible.

Thank you!

Introduction

By Dr. Linda Turner Bynoe

IN THE INTRICATE TAPESTRY of Dudley "Trusty" Bynoe's life—woven with triumph, sorrow, and hardship—there is a common thread: resilience. This memoir chronicles the defining events, the influential people, and the hard-won lessons that shaped Trusty's path, offering a vivid portrait of a man whose life was driven by an unyielding sense of loyalty and a fierce commitment to justice. Like a warrior standing guard at the gates of equity, Trusty faced the battles of systemic racism and prejudice head-on, refusing to waver in the face of adversity. Young firefighters often heard distorted stories of him from white colleagues and a few Black firefighters who never understood him.

The truth of Trusty's impact burned brightly among those who truly knew him. Even in retirement, he remained a pillar of strength—answering calls from young Black firefighters seeking guidance, connecting them to resources, and keeping the flame of hope alive. Trusty maintained an extensive network of Black fire chiefs across the nation, ready to advocate for those navigating the uphill battles of promotions and equity. He took pride in the Santa Clara County Black Firefighters Association's unprecedented success, helping create a legacy that produced the largest number of Black firefighters in the western conference. Trusty was not merely a mentor or advocate; in every sense of the word, he was a warrior, fighting for justice with the pride and conviction of a seasoned champion.

Chapter 1: Trusty introduces readers to his formative years, detailing his young life as a Black child in the Bronx and Port Jefferson Station, Long Island, New York. This chapter delves into the family dynamics, cultural influences, and personal challenges that shaped his future and earned him the nickname "Trusty." Through vivid memories and reflections, it reveals the foundation of the values that defined his life's journey.

Chapter 2: This section captures Trusty's journey as a young man navigating love, ambition, and identity during the 1960s, a time of profound social change. In Seaside, California, he starts a life with Linda Delores Turner, whose partnership becomes a source of shared purpose. This chapter highlights their struggles and sacrifices, setting the stage for a future defined by family, community, and unyielding determination.

Chapter 3: Trusty highlights his entrance into the Emergency Employment Act (EEA) training program, marking his path toward becoming the second Black firefighter hired by the San Jose Fire Department. This chapter explores the personal significance of this milestone, the systemic barriers he faced, and the relationships built with fellow trainees. Set against the social changes of 1971, it captures his resilience and the influence of trailblazers like Chief Robert Osby.

Chapter 4: Trusty recounts a pivotal moment in forming the Santa Clara County Black Firefighters Association (SCCBFA), set against the turbulent backdrop of newly formed social movement organizations. During an organizing meeting that escalated into a life-threatening confrontation, Trusty and his fellow firefighters faced both internal doubts and external threats, solidifying their mission to challenge systemic racism within the fire service. This chapter highlights the courage, sacrifices, and unyielding resolve to create lasting change.

Chapter 5: Trusty explores his experiences at Station 16, where he faced blatant racism while serving East San Jose's predominantly Black and brown communities. Determined to improve the treatment residents received from emergency responders, Trusty encountered discrimination both in the actions of white firefighters and in the training they received. Despite the toxic environment, he found personal growth, solidarity, and respect through his resilience and defiance against systemic injustice. The chapter highlights the disparities in the services provided to residents of East San Jose, revealing the racialized treatment that marginalized communities often receive from public servants. Trusty's interactions with coworkers, law enforcement, and community members deepened his understanding of social responsibility within his profession. Trusty also shares the psychological and emotional impact he felt when he discovered five children dead in a home belonging to a resident known to all the firefighters. His reflections in this chapter address the emotional toll of these experiences and how they shaped his career.

Chapter 6: Trusty captures a pivotal phase in the growth of the SC-CBFA as its second president. Determined to build a stable foundation, Trusty prioritized securing meeting space, recruiting Black firefighters, and empowering future generations of black people to be involved in community activism. Strategic alliances, including partnerships with Angelo Chancellor and the International Association of Black Professional Firefighters (IABPFF), were key to advancing recruitment, training, and advocacy efforts. These efforts culminated in notable achievements, such as the appointment of Robert Osby as San Jose's first Black fire chief in 1985. The chapter also examines challenges within the Firefighters' union, where the author often stood alone as a Black representative who used his political acumen to push for change. Through confrontations and alliances, Trusty evolved from a militant advocate to a skilled strategist, championing racial equity and the advancement of Black firefighters.

Chapter 7: Trusty reflects on his leadership within the SCCBFA and his evolving approach to activism. The narrative underscores his deepening commitment to addressing systemic racism within the fire service, highlighting key moments of tension and conflict, particularly with white firefighters within the union. The chapter details Trusty's bold, sometimes confrontational methods in advocating for Black firefighters' rights, from tackling discriminatory practices in hiring and promotions to pushing for improved overtime pay. His candid recollections of a physical altercation with a fellow firefighter and its emotional toll on his family offer a raw insight into the personal and professional challenges of leadership in a racially divided institution. Despite setbacks, Trusty's efforts would eventually lead to significant changes, further cementing his role as a warrior for Black firefighters.

Chapter 8: Trusty faces the complex collaboration between the San Jose Fire Department and the Local 873/230 union in this chapter. He proposed that the union was only loyal to white firefighters. After a lengthy suspension, he returned to Station 16, only to find shifting perceptions from his crew and union members as tensions rose over his advocacy for racial equity. The chapter highlights his frustrations with the union's resistance to change and conflicts within the SCCBFA. Trusty's decision to enter union politics and push for reforms, such as a Minority Affairs Committee, marks a key moment in his fight against inequities. His efforts to address financial mismanagement and secure fair representation for minority firefighters reflect his commitment to challenging entrenched power structures, despite significant personal costs.

Chapter 9: Trusty explores the SCCBFA's growth, highlighting its expanded role in supporting Black candidate officers in the fire service and the community. During this period, the organization backed trailblazers like Iola Williams and LaDoris Cordell, who made historic strides in local governance and the judiciary. The chapter also covers advanced recruitment practices and community engagement efforts aimed at inspiring the next generation of Black people in Santa Clara County. However, this growth led to internal conflicts, particularly the tension between militant activism and professional development. As more Black firefighters advanced, shifting dynamics within the SCCBFA reflected broader challenges in the fire service, with younger Black members often seeking validation from white colleagues. Despite these struggles, the chapter emphasized the continued commitment to fighting systemic racism and preserving its activist roots.

Chapter 10: "Girl Dad" explores the complexities of fatherhood, identity, and responsibility that Trusty felt in shaping his daughters' lives. The chapter opens with a dramatic rescue in Seaside, where Trusty saved two children from a burning apartment fire—a heroic act that left him both proud and conflicted. Trusty reflects on his evolving relationship with his daughters, Traci and Nicola, and the challenges he faced as they grew into womanhood. From supporting Traci's entrepreneurial spirit to guiding Nicola through personal struggles, Trusty constantly learned what it meant to be a "girl dad." The chapter also highlights the impact of his leadership at Station 16, where he sought to build a community reflecting the values he hoped to instill in my daughters. Looking back, Trusty realizes that while he worked hard to protect and provide for Nicola and Traci, he missed opportunities to be the father they truly needed, particularly as he navigated the intersections of race, gender, and youth.

Chapter 11: Trusty examines pivotal moments in the San Jose Fire Department during a period of leadership transitions and systemic challenges, focusing on Chief Ray Brooks. Brooks's appointment as fire chief brought a new chapter, but it also revealed entrenched resistance to change within the department. The chapter highlights Brook's efforts to address bias in promotional processes, implement merit-based promotions, and support diversity, all while facing a No-Confidence Vote orchestrated by the union. It also explores the roles of figures like Regina Williams and the SCCBFA in navigating these challenges, offering a candid look at the intersection of race, leadership, and institutional accountability.

Chapter 12: Trusty explores a challenging period in his career marked by the civil service hearings and the struggle for a resolution. His reinstatement caused him to rethink his career. Trusty sought support from trusted allies like Captain Marvin Coffee, but the gamesmanship of Engineer Terry Mainzer quickly disrupted any hope for a peaceful work environment. The conflict with Mainzer forced Trusty to confront personal decisions about his future in the fire service. Through battles for disability retirement, the chapter reveals the systemic inequities within the department and the broader societal forces that included retirement pay. The fallout from a violent act by a former fire captain, Grimmenger, further exposed deep divisions within the SCCBFA and the community. These experiences ultimately shaped his final steps about his future.

Chapter 13: In the mid-1990s, a surge of federal cases addressing systemic discrimination set the stage for a pivotal legal battle led by Trusty. As the SCCBFA and its allies confronted deep-rooted racism within the San Jose Fire Department, Trusty spearheaded a federal civil rights lawsuit aimed at dismantling discriminatory practices. This chapter highlights the meticulous preparation, strategic alliances, and resilience behind this legal fight, which exposed divisions within the SCCBFA and the broader Black community. For Trusty and his coplaintiffs, the case was about more than individual justice—it was about affirming the worth of every Black firefighter. The courtroom became a battleground where institutional racism was laid bare, and the limits of justice were tested, marking a historic fight for fairness and equality.

Chapter 14: Trusty explores the emotional toll of public and personal struggles as he faces the fallout from the civil service hearing against the San Jose Fire Department. Amidst a federal discrimination trial, he and his colleagues fight to expose systemic inequities in the fire service. Personal crises arise when Trusty and his wife, Linda, confront her father's illness, leading them to reconsider their future in San Jose. A brief respite in Hilton Head offers Trusty a moment of renewal before he is drawn back into the realities of caregiving and a second federal trial. This chapter highlights their journey of resilience and transformation as they navigate challenges while seeking a new life in Monterey.

Chapter 15: This chapter chronicles a deeply personal and heartbreaking period in his life—the battle against cancer that claimed his beloved daughter Traci. It reflects the raw pain of facing a challenge he couldn't control or solve, unlike the trials he had faced during his career and personal life. As the family united to provide Traci with love and dignity, they confronted a healthcare system that often overlooked Black patients' humanity. This chapter captures the sorrow of losing a child and the strength found in faith, community, and the precious memories shared in her final days. It is a journey through grief, resilience, and the unbreakable bond of a father's love.

Chapter 16: This chapter reflects the joy and camaraderie Trusty found in the years after his mother died, through shared interests and enduring friendships. With golf as a central theme, the greens became a medium for rekindling connections and creating lasting memories. Whether in Southern California with old friends or hosting gatherings during Monterey's vibrant blues and jazz festivals, these experiences exemplify how life's simple pleasures can foster deep bonds and create new traditions. Amid the backdrop of music, culture, and community, Trusty also focused on ensuring his family's well-being, particularly by bringing Nicola closer to them after Traci's passing. These moments of fellowship and family gatherings offered much-needed solace, a reminder that even amid profound loss, fellowship opportunities can be a powerful source of healing.

Chapter 17: This chapter encapsulates Trusty's unwavering zest for life, resilience, and appreciation for human connection. From international travels to Italy and South Africa to facing critical health challenges, Trusty embraced each moment with an adventurous spirit and a sense of purpose. These transformative trips deepened his understanding of history, culture, and shared struggles for justice. As Trusty reflects on his final years, he focuses on family, friendships, and legacy, with a return to Barbados and reunions with old friends symbolizing his commitment to honoring his roots.

Chapter 18: This chapter highlights the joys and significance of travel, family connections, and the camaraderie among retired firefighters. The chapter begins with a memorable family trip to Barbados, celebrating Nicola's fiftieth birthday and reconnecting with distant relatives. It captures the warmth of shared meals, cultural exchanges, and cherished memories. The narrative transitions to the inaugural Retired Black Firefighters Reunion in Las Vegas, a gathering that reinforced bonds among retirees and their families. This chapter also recounts travels across the United States, a romantic getaway to Europe, and reflections on the value of shared experiences. Culminating with the Retired Black Firefighters Reunion in Monterey, the chapter underscores the importance of community, legacy, and celebrating life amidst challenges. Through every journey, Dudley's dedication to fostering unity and preserving connections shines brightly. This chapter beautifully concludes *They Call Me Trusty*, highlighting his enduring spirit and dedication to building bridges that will inspire future generations.

A Brief History

Black Americans, 1920s–1950s

THIS BRIEF HISTORY OF Black America's rise focuses on the discussions among Caribbean immigrants in New York as they arrived in the United States. The event discussed often was the history of O. W. Gurley, a Black man who purchased forty acres of land in Tulsa which he named Greenwood, later called the "Black Wall Street" by Marcus Garvey.[1] Gurley aimed to establish a self-sufficient economic community for Black individuals. He decided to sell his land exclusively to Black Americans, turning down offers from interested white buyers until they were ultimately forced out of their town. Greenwood prospered economically as a thriving Black community, attracting many Black individuals from the South. The town flourished with minimal support from neighboring white communities until a tragic event occurred in 1921.

An accusation arose that a Black man had assaulted a white woman, prompting hundreds from the white community to demand the police hand over the accused for a lynching. Under the inspired leadership of A. J. Smitherman, a dedicated publisher and civil rights activist, the Black community united to protect the young Black man. They gathered in solidarity at the courthouse and jail, determined to stand against injustice and ensure his safety. One could question whether the white residents were defiant or

1. The overview of Gurley's history in Tulsa is drawn from Charles River Editors, *Black Wall Street.*

envious of Greenwood's successes. However, these emotions ignited the worst racial violence in the history of Black massacres.

Many Black lives were lost, homes were destroyed, and military aircraft were deployed to bomb the remnants of the community. This horrific incident left a lasting impact on the psyche of Black and Caribbean people as they navigated across the nation.

During the early 1900s, Black people migrated from southern states to northern regions of the United States in search of a better life, seeking to escape overt racism, segregation, indentured servitude, convict leasing policies, and the brutal realities of Jim Crow laws, including widespread lynching. Simultaneously, many Black people from the Caribbean West Indies immigrated to Harlem, New York, looking for improved financial opportunities. By 1925, 28 percent of Harlem's Black residents were foreign-born.[2] These Caribbean immigrants often arrived with a solid primary education and skilled trades but limited financial resources. They were crucial in establishing community newspapers and financial cooperatives in Harlem and its surrounding boroughs. Their relocation allowed them to thrive independently, as they formed financial institutions despite facing minimal support from white establishments. At the same time, Caribbean immigrants were viewed as hardworking and educated, an exception to Black Americans, which sometimes led to them having better job opportunities than Black migrants from the southern states. However, Caribbean Americans were not treated equally to whites for jobs, housing, and other social interactions.

I grew up in a typical Caribbean family, a people knowledgeable about Black history and the progress made by African Americans in the United States. Like my grandparents, my parents were involved in the Black community. Later, when my parents moved to Harlem, they contributed to building financial opportunities for Black people. Banking was not accessible to Black people in Harlem. However, Black people pooled their money together and established savings accounts or mini banks to help the community build start-up storefronts and small businesses such as horse-pulled carts to sell ice and wood. They participated in establishing inner-city farms and other business prospects that would help improve the neighborhood's health and wealth. Education was necessary, and discussions about improving children's knowledge and establishing Black excellence were held

2. "Russian Jews (480,000) made up the largest foreign-born group in New York, followed by Italian (319,000), Irish (203,450), and German (194,154) immigrants. . . . Between 1917 and 1925, 200,000 African Americans moved to New York." Chen, "What Was Life Like."

everywhere: on stoops, in stores, at work, and in church. Harlem's Black leaders established the Harlem Renaissance, an intellectual and cultural revival of African American music, dance, art, fashion, literature, theater, and politics.

My parents talked about famous Black people who were courageous and creative. My grandparents held conversations in their home with neighbors and friends interested in politics, policies, education, and laws that affected Black people financially and legally. During the 1930s and 1940s, Black newspapers highlighted the efforts and contributions of Black men. When World War II was declared on December 11, 1942, more than one million Black men and women enlisted in every branch of the United States armed forces. The Army, Navy, Air Force, and Marine Corps segregated Black Americans into separate units due to the perception that Black individuals were inferior and less capable than their white counterparts. To compound this indignity, the military often assigned white officers from the South to command Black soldiers, reinforcing these discriminatory beliefs.

My grandparents and their friends were very proud of the military efforts of Black men. Under the leadership of General George S. Patton's army, for example, the 761st tank battalion was singled out and praised for its brave actions in securing France. They were given special commendations for their conspicuous courage, expressing the superior efforts of Black soldiers.

The Associated Negro Press (1919–1964), *Amsterdam News* (established in New York City), *The People's Voice* (also known as *Voice*, which served the African American community and was founded by Adam Clayton Powell in 1941), and the *Chicago Defender* (founded in 1905) were influential in keeping Black people throughout the country, specifically in major northern cities such as New York City, Chicago, and Philadelphia, supplied with information regarding Black men's military achievements. Black communities were well aware of the efforts, contributions, triumphs, and bravery of the Tuskegee Airmen. From 1941 to 1946, one thousand Black pilots were trained at Tuskegee, Alabama. The airmen's success in escorting bombers during WWII had one of the lowest records of lost aircraft of all the escort fighter groups, and they were in constant demand for their service by allied bomber units.[3] Lesser-known Black men also became community heroes when they showed bravery during the war. Dorie Miller was a steward on the USS *West Virginia* during the Japanese attack on Pearl Harbor. On December 7, 1941, without training on the ship's fighting

---

3. Michaeli, *Defender.*

equipment, he operated the machine gun during the attack, held back the initial assault, and saved some wounded sailors by carrying them to safety. He became the first Black American to receive the Navy Cross.[4] This act of bravery prompted civil rights groups to lobby for Black sailors to have more responsibility and respect in the war. Black elders would follow up on these stories, seeking wartime policy changes. The year I was born, 1944, the Navy commissioned the destroyer escort USS *Mason*, the first ship to have a predominantly Black crew.[5]

Many Black soldiers who bravely fought in WWII were surprised to return home to violent white mobs who resented Black Americans in uniform. It was not until July 1948 that President Harry Truman signed Executive Order 9981 to desegregate the US Armed Forces. However, full integration did not occur until the Korean War in 1950. Many Black women of this generation also enlisted in the military. Still, the majority of Black women became the heads of their households to save the lives of their veteran husbands, sons, or brothers as they returned home to extraordinarily hostile and dangerous conditions. These stories about war heroes prompted many Black male youths of my generation to see the military as a way to improve their status and possibly see the world.

The Black community already had its sports giant: boxing. Jack Johnson defeated Tommy Burns in 1908 in the fight of the century. By 1937, Joe Louis, the Brown Bomber, reigned as the world heavyweight champion from 1937 to 1949. He was regarded as the first Black American to achieve the nationwide status of hero in the United States. He not only held the heavyweight championship, but Louis also helped to integrate the game of golf, breaking the sport's color barrier.[6] He was a national hero. These sports figures gave Black male youths an understanding of how their physical acumen was an asset.

Jackie Robinson, at twenty-eight, became the first Black Major League Baseball player in 1947 and signed a contract with the Brooklyn Dodgers. He became a star infielder and outfielder for the Dodgers and the National Leagues' Rookie of the Year. He was inducted into the Baseball Hall of Fame in 1962. After attending the University of California at Los Angeles, where he lettered in four varsity sports—baseball, basketball, football, and track—he joined the army and was commissioned as a second lieutenant. He

---

4. Milton, "Dorie Miller Trophy Award."
5. Schick, "USS *Mason*."
6. Wikipedia, "Joe Louis."

protested instances of racial discrimination during his tour in the military and was court-martialed in 1944. However, he ultimately was honorably discharged. All the boys in my neighborhood looked up to Jackie Robinson and aspired to be like him.[7]

During the early 1950s, many political and legal events gave Black American pre–baby boomers hope for equitable opportunities. Thurgood Marshall successfully argued Brown v. Board of Education in 1954 before the Supreme Court, declaring segregation unconstitutional and illegal in public education. In 1950, Ralph Bunche received the Nobel Peace Prize for the Middle East peace talks, and the National Basketball Association rescinded the color barrier for players. In 1956, Nat King Cole became the first Black person to host a national television show. Lorraine Hansberry in 1961 became the first Black woman to produce the Broadway play *A Raisin in the Sun*.[8] Unfortunately, in retribution for legal and artistic accomplishments, white supremacist groups, such as the neo-Nazis and the Ku Klux Klan, hurled violence and hatred throughout the country, targeting Black Americans. I remember those political discussions among the elders, but I wasn't interested until I read the story about Emmett Till.

Black communities were shocked and appalled when the photograph of the battered and mutilated body of fourteen-year-old Emmett Till's corpse appeared in *Jet* magazine, an African American weekly publication, on August 24, 1955.[9] The mainstream media soon picked up the story and posted it nationwide. I remember the day the photo appeared and the anger and fear that gripped the hearts of so many Black Americans. What did this mean for Black Americans in the United States? Pre–baby boomer Black artists and scholars used their talents to expose the atrocities of the time. Their contributions ultimately influenced the next generation to understand that some white people in the United States of America did not value Black people as human beings. It signaled to young Black men to remain vigilant as they denounced racism and white supremacy.

Throughout my life, even as a child growing up in New York, I have felt a deep responsibility to speak out for justice and to advocate for the voiceless. I do not compare my humble efforts and modest contributions to social justice with the monumental achievements of the heroes and sheroes discussed in the preceding paragraphs. These historic Black heroes lived

7. Henry, "Jackie Robinson."

8. Bogle, *Blacks in American Films*, 11.

9. Library of Congress, "Murder of Emmett Till."

their adult lives during some of the worst times, marked by abject racism, Jim Crow lynchings, and other hateful methods used to confine them to a caste system of fear. While the United States continues to grapple with racism, I have never experienced the pervasive fear that our early Black heroes endured. These historical figures lived in an era when displays of brilliance, dedication, determination, social justice, or physical prowess significantly impacted the next generation in the United States. Their contributions continue to influence all people in the United States thanks to their unwavering commitment and sacrifice in the name of social justice.

Chapter 1

They Call Me Trusty

DUDLEY BYNOE INVITES READERS into the formative years of his life, vividly describing his upbringing as a Black child in the Bronx and later in Port Jefferson, Long Island. This chapter explores how his family dynamics, cultural heritage, and personal struggles shaped the resilient and principled man he became. Dudley reflects on his parents' contrasting influences, the strength of his grandmother's guidance, and the challenges of navigating both familial expectations and systemic inequities.

These early experiences, marked by discipline, adaptability, and an emerging sense of self, laid the foundation for Dudley's values and the nickname "Trusty," which became a defining part of his identity. Through humor, hardship, and poignant memories, this chapter captures the roots of a man determined to rise above adversity.

In 1944, I was born, the second son, the third child of six, to Dudley and Ruby Bynoe in New York City Hospital. Immediately after my birth, the doctor told my mother I had an irregular heartbeat, and I was given a blood transfusion. My heart condition was my mother's concern throughout her life.

The family lived in the Bronx, New York, where I was raised until I was ten. My father, born in Barbados in 1889, was twenty-eight years older than my mother. My mother, born in 1917 in New York City, was a second-generation American; her parents were born in Barbados during the late 1800s. We lived in a tenement building in the Bronx, with a grocery store next door. The store was owned by a Jewish couple, Al and Betty Boyer. They were my parents' friends and ultimately became my godparents, who watched my brothers and me during the day while my parents worked. My mother worked in the janitorial department of New York University (NYU), and my father worked as a bookkeeper for several small businesses. Al and Betty's grandson, Tommy Triptree, would visit his grandparents and play with us during the summer. Growing up in the Bronx, I remember the clean, cobbled streets and tree-lined sidewalks. My brothers and I sometimes played across the street from our apartment in a vacant lot; we called it the silver lot because of the shards of broken glass glittering on the ground in the sunlight.

Next to the grocery store was a liquor store. Instead of playing in the streets, my brothers and I sometimes ran between the stores playing boy games, like cowboys and Indians, or gangsters. One day, while hanging out in the liquor store, I saw a gun, behind the counter, for the first time. I approached the weapon and heard the liquor store owner yelling, "Do not touch that." I remember clearly how stern the store owner was and the lecture he gave me about the danger of guns. The grocery and liquor store owners were the only white people I saw in my neighborhood. Most of the community was Puerto Rican and Black. Growing up in New York was fun. The only bad part was my dad's strictness. He would physically punish us for minor errors. Sometimes, we had to stand in the corner for extended periods; my brother Terry and I would most often be the ones in the corner. We devised a game of who could spit the most and create the fastest dribble. My mother was displeased with this game but often kept our transgressions from my father to avoid further punishment.

My father had high expectations for his children; he was a disciplinarian. We had to learn to tie our neckties and polish our shoes at a very young age to appear appropriate when going to church or visiting my parents' friends. On the other hand, my mother was a caring, loving person who gave in to her children's whims. At the age of three, she enrolled me in a nursery school because I was too much to handle; I was demanding and cried a lot. My father felt the money spent on special education for me was unnecessary, yet my mother prevailed. I recall an incident in kindergarten where a boy named Johnny Bennet tried to take my lunch. We started fighting. I was beating him up until he bit me. I remember yelling at him, "YOU BIT ME." In my house, when my brothers and I fought, biting was against the rules.

Life became heartbreaking and insecure when my parents were separated and later divorced. The four oldest boys—George, Winston, Terry, and I—were moved to Port Jefferson, Long Island, to live with my grandparents, Bertha and Clifford Archer. The culture shock of moving to Port Jefferson was overwhelming. This small town was predominantly white, with only ten to fifteen Black families residing there. My grandparents were among the first Black families to purchase land and build a house in Port Jefferson Station during the late 1950s.

The house and land owned and built by my grandparents was a two-bedroom, one-bath home with a large attic that became the boys' room and a detached garage. My grandparents owned several acres of land where they grew vegetables and fruit and raised a few farm animals. A windmill was perched on top of the detached garage. The windmill was scary, adding to my concerns about moving to Port Jefferson. Then there was Granny, the head of the household; she did not work outside of the home. She had a solid Bajan accent and was very strict but not as harsh or hurtful as my dad. She generally would warn you before you got beaten with a belt. I thought Granny was a wise old lady; she taught me much about life. She took me under her wing because I quickly figured out how to please her. I worked in the kitchen, read the Bible, and sang songs to her. Granny would tell me how much she loved my imagination. I was unsure what she meant, but she thought my ideas were innovative; I could figure out different ways to conquer a task. My brother's chores were weeding the gardens, feeding the farm animals, and cleaning their pens throughout the year. I also had to do farm chores during the hot summer months, and I hated it. I hung out mainly with Granny. Once, I did something that angered her. She became so disturbed by my behavior that she threatened me with Bajan voodoo. Granny told me if I misbehaved again (I do not remember what I did), she would make my feet swell up, and I would not be able to walk again. I believed her and never again misbehaved in the same manner.

Now that my father was out of our lives and no longer available to me, I welcomed a relationship with Mr. Dorsett, the father of my best friend, Johnny. Johnny was always one inch taller and ten pounds heavier than me. We were like brothers, staying at each other's homes, playing with cap guns, ball games, and other boy games. My grandmother's home was next door to the Dorsett family house. Down the street lived my aunt, my mother's younger sister, and her seven children, my cousins. The neighborhood was tight. Most of the Black families owned their own homes, and all the children stayed in the neighborhood. Of course, my cousins were substantially younger than me, so we did not play together, but all Jayne Boulevard families came together for celebrations and holidays. Holiday meals consisted of freshly baked coconut bread, collard greens, ham, macaroni and cheese, fresh corn, and often saltwater cod, which I did not like. Drinks consisted of Kool-Aid and sweet tea, with Granny's layered cake. My favorite was the pineapple upside-down cake. Granny insisted that we eat everything she put on our plates. I would put those items I did not like in my pockets to avoid being scolded by Granny. We did not dare lie to Granny, even about minor things, but she seldom asked whether we ate our food. She just looked for empty plates.

Granny shared information about her life in Barbados; she would explain the differences in the spirit of religion, church, and education. She was concerned about the people she loved, which inspired many neighbors and family friends to seek her wisdom. She counseled anyone who requested her point of view. She valued truth and expected her family to always do the honest and right thing. Her knowledge would often be expressed through parables such as, "If you lie down with dogs, you will get up with fleas," "Cat luck is not dog luck," "People take advantage of those who are weak," and "Good and evil can never live peacefully together." We were encouraged to make an impression wherever we went and on all levels of life. It was not until I visited Barbados as an adult and connected with my Bajan cousins that I learned that Granny had left a daughter in Barbados when she immigrated to the United States. Of course, Granny's generation was the generation of family secrets, too. My family in Barbados was highly educated and accomplished. They are not tall like me; they are small in stature but have tremendous athletic abilities.

Granny was very strict about education and had high expectations for her grandchildren. We were told that the educational system in Barbados was considered a better system than the United States. The evidence was its higher literacy rate. Barbados was known for its excellent education programs and the respected and highly educated teachers in their communities. The country was primarily Black, with fewer anti-Black racist attitudes toward its youth. Of course, Barbados has a substantially smaller population than the United States, even small compared to Long Island, which allowed teachers to provide personalized attention to their students.

The educational system on Long Island was also more advanced than New York City schools. My brothers and I quickly learned that advanced academic skills were needed to meet Long Island students' levels. My sister, Bertha, lived with my grandmother several years before us boys. I wanted to know how long she lived on Long Island before we moved there or why she was sent there first. However, the secret was never revealed to me. Bertha had adapted well to the Long Island school systems. She was an A student and ultimately became the valedictorian of her high school class. My brothers were able to catch up to their grade level with my sister's help.

On the other hand, at ten years old, I was assigned to the fifth grade. The teacher was a slacker. He just sat behind his desk and allowed the students to play or do whatever they pleased. I never had homework my brothers or sister could help me with. They either thought I was a genius or lying about the teacher. After the fifth grade, I fell even further behind my peers, sisters, and brothers. The oldest of my siblings would review my homework and assess my grades. My sister would inform my grandmother about my lack of knowledge and discipline. My brothers constantly teased me because of my grades. I believe I was left behind in seventh grade, which made it unbearable to deal with the barrage of insults and lack of sibling support. My grandmother and mother never doubted my intelligence, but they could not determine how best to help me with school.

At least once a month, my mother traveled with my youngest brother, Myles, to Port Jefferson Station on the train to visit us. She brought bags of clothes, food, and sometimes toys. Ma was always tired when she arrived, but she dedicated time to each of us, questioning our progress in school and checking out our friends. Our life was seldom exciting. Growing up as a young Black boy on Jayne Boulevard, where there were a few homes, an extensive woodsy area, and close family and friends, was all I knew until I bought my first car. My mother always encouraged me to read and try new things. She frequently told me if you can read, you can learn anything. I was always a reader.

There were several highly shocking racist events happening in the United States during my young years. My granny was religious yet aware of the United States' politics against Black people, especially Black boys. She worried about me and would try her best to build my self-esteem. I remember Granny showing me a photo of Emmett Till and explaining the importance of staying out of trouble and out of the limelight. She encouraged us to stay with our people—as in, only hanging out with Black kids in our neighborhood. I wasn't encouraged to study, but one teacher liked me and chose me to be the class trustee, stating I was the most honest student. I never lied to her or made excuses for not completing my homework. Being assigned the position of class trustee was an honor I held proudly. It was the name my classmates called me; thus, it became my nickname. To this day, all of my friends and some of my family address me as Trusty.

However, for many reasons, school remained an issue. I found it challenging to catch up with my siblings or my assigned class year after year. I wanted and needed friends with whom I could compete and who valued my inherent talents. So, when I turned sixteen, I asked my grandmother to allow me to quit school and go to work. She knew I could work because, for years, I worked a part-time job as a paper carrier and on a chicken farm during the summers. Granny approved my request; I could leave school under the agreement that I stayed home until I turned eighteen, paid rent, and saved money. Granny opened a Christmas club account at the bank, where I had to save twenty-five dollars and pay twenty-five dollars rent monthly. Granny expected me to work hard and continue to learn independently. My main reason for working was to buy clothes. I always hated wearing hand-me-down clothes from my oldest brother. Our personalities and fashion styles were very different. I wanted the latest, most current styles; George's style was conservative and traditional.

MY SIBLINGS

My sister, Bertha, was the oldest and did not grow up with us in the Bronx. She often acted more like a mother than a sister, being quite bossy and seldom engaging in profound or meaningful conversations with me. Before we left for school or church, she meticulously inspected the boys' clothing, teeth, ears, and shoes. Bertha kept her distance from me, and it was clear I was not her favorite brother. I remember Granny mentioning that Bertha had a photographic memory. She married young and had two children, a boy and a girl, and later earned a bachelor's degree.

My relationships with my brothers were often strained. George, the oldest boy, and I were never close. My mother said we fought from the cradle to adulthood. He always won the fights I started. George was domineering, believed he knew everything, and tried to control everyone around him. He joined the Navy and eventually earned a bachelor's degree in mechanics. George married several times. I attended his first and third weddings, both of which were elegant. To my knowledge, he never had any children.

My brother Winston was a year and a half younger than me. He was a scholar and a great wrestler during high school. After quitting school, I would attend Winston's wrestling matches and cheer him on. Winston also played the tuba, and Johnny and I used to tease him about it. Winston and I were friendly with each other. He never thought I was dumb; he was in awe of my ability to find work and make money. He grew up to be a minister and husband and fathered three sons and one daughter. He received a degree in business. Winston's wife, Edna, was a lovely woman who died in the 1980s, leaving the entire family grieving. Edna was the first family member of our generation to die, leaving us wondering who would be next. Winston married several times after Edna's death.

Terry was my favorite brother. He was three years younger, a good athlete with a daring personality. Terry always did things to irritate Granny. He had this trick with his eyelids that looked spooky and freaky. He would turn his eyelids inside out. I told him not to let Granny see him do his trick, but of course, the daring Terry one day decided to do his trick in front of Granny. Granny immediately sent him back to our mother in New York City. That was one of the saddest days in my young life. I tried to persuade Granny to let Terry stay, even promising I would stop him from doing his eye tricks. However, Granny was superstitious and would not yield to my pleadings. The move to New York, I believe, hurt Terry too. He had grown to adulthood in New York City, caring for our youngest brother, Myles, while our mother worked at night. Surrounded by drugs and crime, he eventually fell into the grip of alcohol. When Terry was old enough, he joined the army and went to Vietnam, where he was hit by shrapnel from an explosion near his dugout. During his stay in the army hospital, he received several blood infusions and serious drugs to manage his pain, which led to an addiction. Despite these challenges, my brothers were talented and had a unique resilience, allowing them to lift themselves from difficult situations and persevere. Terry eventually overcame his addiction, went to college, earned a bachelor of arts in business administration, and secured a prestigious position at the US Department of Housing and Urban Development. Although he never married, he maintained healthy relationships with several women.

I did not grow up with my youngest brother, Myles, as he was only seven when I was sent to live with Granny. As a teenager, I would take the Long Island Rail Road, or drive when I had a car, to see my mother in New York City. During these visits, Myles seemed happy to see me, his older brother. Myles was an intellectual who also played baseball. I was incredibly proud of him when he earned a full Massachusetts Institute of Technology (MIT) scholarship to study philosophy. The summer before he started at MIT, he spent time with me in California, and we had a wonderful time together. I even put his books away in the attic to ensure he wouldn't just stay indoors reading. I wanted us to hang out, get to know each other, and enjoy each other's company.

Unexpectedly, Myles fell in love with Linda's younger sister, Leonora, and didn't want to leave California. He wanted to stay, get a job, and pursue a relationship with her. Since I never had the opportunity to go to college, I insisted that he not give up the chance to have a better life. To this day, I wish I had recognized Myles's dilemma or could have predicted the future. After several years, Myles graduated from MIT with honors and earned two master's degrees in philosophy and law. However, when he moved back to New York City, he faced challenges that led to him becoming homeless, despite the family's meaningful efforts to help him. He remained homeless for his entire adult life, and the reasons for his homelessness remain unclear.

I do not know if Myles is alive today. The last time I saw him was a few days after our mother's death. I was in New York City buying a pair of shoes for Linda to wear to the funeral. It was a cold day in November 2006 when I stopped in a bar on Times Square. The bar had windows around the entire lower half of the building, so I could see the street. Myles was one of the homeless people who walked by the window. At first, I was not sure it was Myles, but I felt in my heart it was him. So, I asked the bartender to watch my drink and went outside. I called out to Myles, and he turned around. It was my younger brother. I hugged Myles and told him that our mother had died, I tried to convince him to come to the house, where I would help him clean up and provide him with the appropriate clothes to wear to the funeral. Myles never came to Ma's house, and I never saw him again. My sister-in-law Leonora was never as happy as she was with Myles. She died of cancer at the young age of thirty-four.

I DROP OUT OF SCHOOL

At sixteen, I started wearing a conk. During the late 1950s and 1960s, the conk hairstyle was popular among Black men with naturally kinky hair. Many barbershops in the United States have at least one barber specializing in conking hair, which involves straightening it. The name "conk" is derived from Congolese, and it consisted of a gel of potatoes, eggs, and lye. As I developed my style, my conk and fashionable clothes became a beacon for girls, sparking a new source of interest for me. Stylishness was always important to me, even during the 1970s when Afros became popular. I wore an enormous Afro. And, like many Black men, my hair became a symbolic protest for social justice, equal rights, and Black pride. To dress in the latest fashion, I needed a job.

My uncle Vincent (Vinney) Morrison, a Jamaican man, was married to my aunt Margie, my mother's younger sister. He had a successful business, polishing cars. He had multiple contracts with car dealerships throughout Suffolk County, Long Island. Vinney even owned a speedboat docked at the Port Jefferson Yacht Club. Uncle Vinney gave me my first full-time paying job as his assistant. I earned one hundred dollars cash a week in 1961. That was a lot of money for a sixteen-year-old Black male. Vinney taught me a lot about working hard and being a man. He taught me about women; he believed in having girlfriends. Granny's Christmas club savings account yielded me five hundred dollars in savings by the time I was eighteen. My uncle Vinney helped me buy my first car in 1961, wholesale for five hundred dollars, a 1957 black convertible Ford Fairlane. I thought I was the shit until I totaled the car on a snowy highway one evening while on a date with my girlfriend.

After working for Uncle Vinney for a year, the business faced a 50 percent decline due to increased competition from similar companies established by white entrepreneurs. Uncle Vinney could not afford to keep me on full time at my pay scale. I got another job as an orderly for the state of New York at Kings Park Psychiatric Center in Kings Park County, forty minutes south of Port Jefferson Station. The pay was not as good, but the work hours were decent. I worked there for a year. I found the job depressing; so many young people were locked up with little hope of ever getting out. To have fun and experience a more unburdened life, I started hanging out with guys who lived in Gordon Heights, thirty minutes south of Port Jefferson Station. Gordon Heights was a poorer, underprivileged Black town. Some of my friends were gangsters, a life I found exciting or at least interesting. Unfortunately, a fight broke out at a grind-them-up party, where teenage boys and girls danced to slow music as they rubbed their bodies together in a grinding motion. During the altercation between two friends, I was pushed through a window, and my left arm was severely cut. I had to spend three months at my mother's apartment in New York City recuperating, attending doctor's appointments and therapy sessions. My mother insisted that I join the army. She was concerned about the friends I was hanging out with.

I was drafted into the United States Army in 1962, but due to my injuries, I did not report for basic training until 1963. My primary training took place at Fort Dix, New Jersey. At the end of preliminary training, draftees were given a questionnaire to determine their active-duty assignments after basic training. I called my oldest brother, George, who was in the Air Force stationed in Spain, for advice. He advised me not to choose the southern states because of the Civil Rights Movement, and suggested that I request Europe or California instead. Ultimately, I was assigned to active duty in California in 1964.

I was stationed at Fort Ord, California, the primary training center for the Vietnam War. The war concerned Black soldiers because statistics for Black men's survival were disturbing. Many young soldiers in my battalion were killed in a battle shortly before my term of duty ended. I feared Vietnam and planned to leave the army as soon as possible, only planning to serve the mandatory two years. The army offered General Education Development (GED) classes and strongly encouraged me to obtain a high school diploma. I completed the GED program with ease.

A heartwarming image of Trusty with his siblings.

Chapter 2

My Girl

CHAPTER 2 OFFERS AN intimate glimpse into Dudley's journey as a young man navigating the complexities of love, ambition, and identity during the 1960s—a time marked by profound social change and personal challenges. In Seaside, California, he finds a home among fellow Black military families and a kindred spirit in Linda Delores Turner. Their elopement in 1965 signals the start of a partnership defined by resilience, dreams, and the shared determination to carve out a better life for their growing family.

This chapter traces the couple's evolving journey, from the struggles of financial instability and the dangers of a community impacted by addiction to the spiritual solace Dudley found at the Still Point retreat. Through moments of separation and reconciliation, Dudley and Linda's bond remains tethered to their shared love for their daughters and their unwavering commitment to uplift themselves and the Black community. Their choices and sacrifices during this period lay the foundation for a future that will challenge and redefine their notions of family, identity, and purpose.

After concluding a demanding two-year military assignment at Fort Ord, I chose to remain in a community that was not only the home of fellow Black military families but also a landscape punctuated by the challenges of poverty, crime, and the looming specter of addiction. It was here, amid the complexities of life and love, that I met Linda Delores Turner. Our impulse to elope to Mexico in 1965 marked the beginning of a shared journey defined by deep bonds, dreams, and the weight of familial expectations. As we prepared to welcome our first child, we confronted the stark reality of financial instability and the dangers nearby, witnessing how drugs affected our community and came to define too many lives around us. With grit and determination, we harnessed our youthful idealism and sought new opportunities beyond Seaside, ultimately laying the foundation for a life that would outlast the shadows of our circumstances. This chapter explores our evolution from newlyweds dreaming of a brighter future to parents navigating the complexities of family life, all while striving to carve out a safe and nurturing space for our children amidst the chaos of a rapidly changing world.

I decided to stay in Seaside, California. Seaside was a small town, primarily home to Black military families due to its proximity to the army base. Although I wasn't drawn to the military's indoctrination, the harsh conditions at Camp Roberts, or the exposure to toxins, the army brought me something precious: my wife, Linda Delores Turner. We eloped to Mexico in 1965 before my service ended, a decision that sparked resistance from both of our families. Yet despite these challenges, Linda and I were deeply in love, bound by a shared vision for the future, but we needed a purpose and a little support. We had so much in common that, at times, our ideas often felt like one. Linda's theatrical sensibility helped me envision a different way of knowing, living, and being. The differences in our desires, thoughts, and actions were minor. I could not believe that Linda understood my needs so well, and I knew I would eventually come to understand hers.

We saw ourselves as free-thinking young Black people of the 1960s, living spontaneously and without limits. But, like many young couples, we were hindered by a lack of financial stability. Our love was strong, but as we prepared for the birth of our first daughter, Nicola Desharn, in 1966, the reality of providing for a family set in. I struggled to find work in Monterey County, and Linda, despite her best efforts, found it difficult to help her mother and sisters as her parents separated and the family faced challenging times. Linda worried because the town of Seaside was plagued by drugs and crime, and several of her school friends fell victim to drug addiction and death.

Seaside, like many towns during the sixties, was not immune to the growing drug epidemic that ravaged military communities. With the counterculture movement and the Vietnam War as a backdrop, drugs like marijuana, cocaine, crack cocaine, and heroin devastated neighborhoods that relied heavily on Fort Ord's economic influence. The small town bore witness to the tragic consequences of addiction, leaving scars that were hard to forget.

As much as we wanted to improve our status, merely making ends meet in Seaside was nearly impossible. I expanded my job search beyond Monterey County and found work at the Ford Motor Company in San Jose. For ninety days, I hitchhiked seventy miles each way from Seaside to Milpitas to complete my probationary period. Though the commute was grueling, I showed up to work on time. When my workday was over at two thirty in the afternoon, I hitchhiked home, ready to hang out with my young family.

During the end of my probationary time, I started looking for a home in San Jose. I was lucky to meet a young Black guy, Arthur Dewitt, a Ford employee, who had bought a house in South San Jose and was moving out of an affordable small duplex. Dewitt agreed to introduce me to the property owner and vouch for our reliability. The duplex owner was an older Black couple well-known in San Jose as politically influential and as owners of several properties in the area. Linda and I dressed as best we could for the interview with Mr. and Mrs. Ribbs, our soon-to-be landlords, who accepted our offer and appeared to like us. Within a few months, another Black family moved into one of the duplexes across from us, Mammie and Willy Wade, with their four children, two boys and two girls; we became good neighbors and friends for many years. Our second daughter, Traci Roquel, was born in San Jose in November 1967.

THE FORD MOTOR COMPANY WORK EXPERIENCE

Most young Black men performing manual labor at Ford Motor Company during the 1960s relieved their work tension by hanging out late with the guys, gambling, drinking, and getting high. Life in San Jose came with its own set of trials. The city, like much of the country, was marred by systemic racism. Discriminatory hiring practices, housing restrictions, and a predominantly white police force made it hard for Black men to thrive. San Jose, many times larger than Seaside, offered few opportunities for Black people, and I faced constant pressure at work. Eventually, tensions boiled over when a foreman physically pushed me, and after a physical altercation, I lost my job.

Losing my job left me frustrated, angry, and desperate; Linda, carrying the weight of our family's emotional burdens, left our home in San Jose in early 1968 and moved back to Seaside to help her mother and to gain support in caring for our daughters. Throughout this turmoil, Linda and I remained friends, although we could not figure out how to live together. We established a ritual of talking every Sunday morning for an hour, regardless of where we lived, whom we lived with, or what we were doing. Moving to New York was never an option. My New York family was very conservative, and I knew Linda and I could never adhere to their traditional religious beliefs. I needed to figure out how to survive. Unforgivably, I yielded to living the life of a low-level gangster for about a year until I stumbled onto Still Point.

During this period of upheaval, I turned to Zen Buddhism, seeking solace and self-reflection at a retreat called Still Point in the Santa Cruz mountains on Bear Creek Road in Los Gatos. There, I met Gia-fu Feng, the commune's founder, who became a mentor to me. My time at Still Point was healing, but it couldn't fill the void of not having a connection to Black culture and community. I was haunted by memories of the brutal injustices perpetrated against Black men, like the horrific killing of Emmett Till, which had been a life-altering moment for many Black folks. The assassinations of Medgar Evers, Malcolm X, and Martin Luther King Jr. were fresh wounds that reminded me of the ongoing fight for civil rights. Gia-fu was impressed with my insight into human behaviors and my distinct ability to read people, both men and women. He saw my strength as a streetwise Black man who could help others face their realities. He knew that at twenty-five, I had a very different cultural experience.[1] Some of the young people at Still Point were from extremely wealthy families, so their concepts of life were very different, yet they were confused about their life's purpose. At the same time, I was genuinely trying to present myself as a wise Black man in white America. Linda seldom visited me at Still Point, although she saw improvement in my attitude and willingness to listen. Linda and I continued to talk weekly; the topics included politics, the problems of living in Seaside, our educational possibilities, and personal hopes and dreams. She even understood the free-love attitude of many of the patrons of Still Point and never asked about my participation, nor did she talk about her friends.

---

1. Wilson, *Still Point*, 151. Carol Ann Wilson's account describes my own attitude while living at Still Point.

Another conflict I had living with white people at Still Point's communal setting was my awareness that Black people throughout the country were fighting for their civil rights, social justice, and the mere survival and progression of the race. I constantly read books written by historical Black authors, and like my mother, I read several daily newspapers. I knew of the horrors and brutality perpetrated on young Black men throughout the United States. I remember incidences when Black racist attitudes and discrimination affected me in New York. Linda could see through my sorrow and helped me bridge the gap between my feelings, my need to grow personally and spiritually, and my desire to make a difference in the world. We could talk about any- and everything. We had different dreams; sometimes, I tried to limit Linda's lofty ideas. But at the end of our conversations, we always discussed providing a better life for our daughters.

The Black Panther Party had established a vision in California and, in 1967, marched on the California State Capitol, armed with guns to protest police brutality. Knowledge of these events further complicated my interactions with white people. During Still Point encounter groups, I would express my pain and the conflict of explaining the devastation of being Black in white America. Some white Jewish members talked about their concerns about White Anglo-Saxon Protestants (WASPs) and their battle with injustice perpetrated in their establishments. These encounters helped me grasp the severe illness white people had, based on the fear of losing their privilege and power positions. However, I was mindful that Still Point could not give me the connection to Black history, Black culture, Black community, and Black pride that had always been important to me. The desire to lift Black communities, help brothers, and help my own family seemed, at times, an impossible task, one that I had to address or lose my soul and my family forever.

By 1971, at the age of twenty-seven, I persuaded Linda to give living together another try. She was juggling two part-time jobs while living in San Francisco, as neither of us could earn enough money in Monterey County to support our daughters. We agreed that if this second attempt didn't work out, we would divorce amicably and find ways to co-parent. Although our marriage was never traditional, I believed it was worth saving. I felt that our efforts to unite our family were essential; it was about having a relationship with my daughters.

Reflecting on my childhood, I remembered playing sports and noticing that while the white kids' fathers were always cheering them on, the Black kids' fathers were seldom present. I wanted my daughters to know me and be proud of their heritage. Linda appreciated my spontaneity, boldness, humor, commitment to Black history and culture, and resilience. I delighted in making her laugh, especially since she often seemed so serious. For many years, "My Girl," the song by The Temptations, perfectly captured how I felt about her. She enjoyed my singing and thought I had a smooth voice, so throughout the years, I serenaded her on special occasions. My vocal talent had blossomed while singing to my grandmother and performing in her church.

Linda was a devoted blues fan, a genre that mirrored her soulful spirit. Coming from a remarkably talented musical family, she grew up with blues and jazz as the preferred genres. Her great-uncle, Willie Dixon, is still renowned worldwide for his contributions to American music. While I appreciated those genres, I also enjoyed the newer sounds of R&B and Motown.

Linda wanted to feel safe and for our daughter to have those things she never could have. Although she never demanded that I change, she carefully offered new career ideas that would help us prosper. Linda always planned for the future; she believed in goal setting and the value of continuous improvement. Respect for our marriage and each other allowed us to grow in our own space. Our dedication to civil rights and human rights never wavered. We continued to profess the motto "By any means necessary," true Malcolm X believers. Linda started working at Pacific Bell, and I started investigating seriously lifelong career opportunities. I had two career choices to think about and resolve.

My mentor at Still Point, Gia-fu Feng, offered me a position as a counselor at Esalen in Big Sur, California. The second opportunity I found in the San Jose *Mercury* newspaper. It was an opportunity to become a San Jose Fire Department firefighter trainee. Throughout the United States, fire departments were sued for their lack of diversity, and the cases lost in court forced cities and municipalities to abide by consent decrees. I perceived that the San Jose Fire Department hired people of color to integrate their department and avoid a consent decree. In retrospect, the San Jose Fire Department only wanted Black men who would acculturate to their white ideology and help secure federally funded programs.

After deliberating with Linda, I decided to choose the fire department. I believed my service in the army would look good on the application. It was a decision that would alter the course of our lives for better or worse.

A nostalgic snapshot of Trusty and Linda showcasing the spirit of the sixties.

A Brief History

1970s Employment Conditions for Black Americans

THE 1970S WERE A turbulent time for Black men in the United States job market. Unemployment among Black men was significantly higher than among their white counterparts. According to the Bureau of Labor Statistics, the average annual unemployment rate for Black men aged twenty and over hovered around 12.3 percent, more than double the rate of the 5.8 percent for white men.[1] These statistics, however, only scratch the surface of the broader economic struggles Black communities faced, which also included underemployment, wage disparity, and discrimination in both hiring and promotion.

To address this economic crisis, legislation such as the Emergency Employment Act (EEA) of 1971 and the Comprehensive Employment and Training Act (CETA) of 1973 were enacted. These laws provided federal funding to local governments, nonprofits, and businesses to create jobs, particularly in areas like construction, public service, and healthcare. The Emergency Jobs and Unemployment Assistance Act of 1974 extended unemployment benefits, provided public service jobs, and allocated special assistance for workers not eligible for standard unemployment benefits. These initiatives were designed to alleviate the devastating effects of high unemployment, inflation, and recession during the 1970s.

---

1. Westcott, "Blacks in the 1970's," table 4.

In San Jose, the 1970 census showed a population of 445,779, of which 93.6 percent were white, including 15.1 percent of Spanish origin.[2] Only. 2.5 percent of the population was identified as Black, and the city's institutions, including the fire department, reflected this racial imbalance. The San Jose Fire Department, like many public institutions at the time, operated within a framework of systemic racism, which marginalized Black people and other minorities. One of the ways this inequality was perpetuated was through the inclusion of Latinos under the broader white demographic, obscuring the true extent of racial inequity in census data. Many Latinos, distancing themselves from their heritage, did not see this as a problem, further contributing to a gap in cultural identity across generations.

In response to these issues, the City of San Jose sought to diversify its workforce, leveraging federal programs like the EEA and CETA to recruit firefighters of color. While these initiatives were a step forward, they required more than just hiring minorities; they needed a cultural shift within the city to truly embrace diversity. I joined the San Jose Fire Department through one of the first such programs, embarking on a journey to confront the long-standing racial barriers within the institution and to fight for equity and justice.

2. Bay Area Census, "City of San Jose."

Chapter 3

Trusting My Gut

IN A WORLD WHERE courage is not just a requirement but a way of life, the journey toward becoming a firefighter often transcends the boundaries of physical endurance and technical skill. It is a voyage laden with personal significance, cultural hurdles, and extraordinary resilience. This chapter unfolds the compelling narrative of his entrance into the EEA training program, a pivotal moment that not only marked a new chapter in Dudley's life but also set the stage for groundbreaking changes within the San Jose Fire Department.

As the second Black firefighter hired in the department's history, Trusty's story is intertwined with themes of family security and the fight against systemic barriers. It was 1971, a time teetering on the edge of social upheaval and change, where every day posed unique challenges as he navigated the complexities of race within an institution largely dominated by a white male majority. Here, Trusty reflects on the struggles and triumphs encountered during his training period, chronicling the relationships formed with fellow trainees from diverse backgrounds and the critical role played by pioneers like Booker T. Law.

In 1971, I became the first African American accepted into the Santa Clara County EEA program, joining a diverse group of twelve trainees. Among them was Jerry, another Black man with whom I formed the closest bond. I also became friends with Tom, a Filipino American; Joe, a Latino American;

and Doug, a white American. Jerry and I later became founding members of the Santa Clara County Black Firefighters Association (SCCBFA).

Based on the San Jose Fire Department's reputation, Black men were expected to endure racist attitudes during training, and I was no exception. As an EEA trainee, I often felt hated and isolated, facing open resentment from many presumed colleagues. At several stations, when I walked into a room, firefighters quickly left. Sometimes, they wouldn't even acknowledge my presence, but the few who did interact with me kept the conversation brief, never extending beyond pleasantries like, "How's the job going?" They never inquired about my family or helped me understand job requirements. Even when riding on the tailboard of the fire engine en route to an emergency call, the firefighter next to me remained silent. The only person who engaged with me was the captain, and even then, only in the context of our work.

However, no one directed overt racist statements at me, likely because I was taller, bigger, and louder than most men. However, there were constant, subtle remarks against people of color that enraged me. I did my best to maintain composure, knowing that finishing the program was crucial. But the stress weighed heavily on me, both at work and at home. I knew that this hostile environment affected not just me but other firefighters of color, who also dealt with racial slurs, exclusion, and a lack of support.

Throughout my career, many firefighters of color complained about the fire department's racist work environment. In some cases, white firefighters who were officers denied opportunities to people of color for professional development, training, or advancement, which limited career growth and earning potential.

However, the training officer was the only person required to interact and communicate daily with the EEA trainees; he assigned the station schedules and training exercises. I never had a problem with the training officer. Permanent firefighters and chief officers gave EEA trainees the label EEA boys. This microaggressive act stigmatized and culturally marginalized us; at the time, I was twenty-seven years old and understood the meaning of boy. There were occasions when EEA trainees were required to do menial tasks, such as washing the chief's cars at the training center. Many firefighters felt EEA trainees did not belong or deserve the job and dared to openly make statements such as, "You don't belong here," "You are not qualified," and "You don't deserve the job." However, they never said the N-word in my presence. Even Latino firefighters, who I initially believed would show solidarity, treated us with disdain. Many even distanced themselves from their Mexican heritage, insisting they were of Spanish descent. The Latino trainees in our group, however, were in a different situation. They faced similar challenges but received assistance from full-time Mexican firefighters. For example, they received help from other Mexican firefighters in passing the civil service exam—a level of support that Jerry and I didn't have, as there were no established Black firefighters in the San Jose Fire Department at that time. Booker Law was the only permanent Black firefighter in the department and was new to the team. He felt it was important to maintain some distance from us to protect his job security. Once, he visited the training center to offer encouragement to Jerry and me, letting us know that he was available if we needed support. We understood that he had good intentions, but we also recognized that forming a friendship with him could jeopardize his position.

Training was tough, but I was determined. We trained and practiced using all the equipment on the fire engines, and we worked hard to pass the physical agility test. At the training center, we focused on learning essential firefighting skills and fire station protocols. We became familiar with all the equipment on the fire engine, such as the pump, water tank, and hose bed containing various hose sizes. Additionally, we trained on setting up and climbing different-sized ladders, maneuvering hundred-foot aerial ladders, quickly donning self-contained breathing apparatus gear, and utilizing various forcible entry tools like axes, pry bars, Jaws of Life, and other devices. Near the end of the two-year training program, we had to pass the physical agility and written test to become full-time firefighters. The physical agility test was as expected. We had trained consistently for the physical agility test, which included assessments titled Stair Climbing, Hose Drag Equipment, Carrying Ladder Raise, Extend Forcible Entry Search, Rescue Ceiling Breaches and Pulls, Medical Emergency Techniques, and First Aid and CPR.

The written test was a civil service examination specifically designed for the fire department. However, it included numerous questions that had little relevance to the training we had received. Both Jerry and I did not pass the test. Upon reviewing the content, we determined that the exam was culturally biased. Many of the questions were unrelated to our practical training and were laden with technical jargon and concepts that were unfamiliar to us. It became clear that the exam was tailored for individuals who had the opportunity, socioeconomic background, and specialized knowledge of advanced mechanical equipment. The questions not only deviated from the skills we had been trained in but also fell outside our cultural experiences. To answer the questions effectively, a prior familiarity with the equipment referenced in the exam was required.

Jerry and I understood that this issue extended beyond our own experience; it highlighted a larger problem of systemic bias in testing. We realized that many young Black males from our generation might not have had the chance to familiarize themselves with questions related to drill presses, lathes, or other complex mechanical equipment.

After our failure on the written exam, the fire department informed us that we had only a few weeks to familiarize ourselves with the equipment before we could retake the test. This raised concerns about the fairness of being required to pass an exam on subjects we had never been trained in. Jerry and I began researching test development and discovered that certain assessments had disproportionately high failure rates for specific groups. We found numerous cases where culturally biased exams unfairly disadvantaged people of color, particularly in professions historically dominated by white men. These exams were designed and administered in ways that systematically disadvantaged individuals from different racial, ethnic, linguistic, or socioeconomic backgrounds than the dominant group. They often included questions or formats unfamiliar or irrelevant to these groups, leading to inaccurate, unjust, and invalid assessments of their abilities and potential.

During the 1970s and 1980s, various social justice organizations raised concerns about the widespread use of culturally biased testing. This issue extended across many sectors, impacting the Scholastic Aptitude Test (SAT) for high school students, as well as other job-related and educational assessments such as intelligence, achievement, aptitude, personality, and standardized tests used in both employment and clinical settings. The consequences were severe for underserved and underrepresented populations, as these biased tests restricted opportunities, perpetuated inequality, reinforced prejudices, and undermined the validity and reliability of the assessments.

To create and evaluate tests that are culturally fair, valid, and reliable, it is crucial to account for cultural diversity and the context of the test takers. Once Jerry and I understood the broader implications of test quality, we strongly believed we had a legitimate case and sought legal representation to challenge the exam. We approached Ed Newman, a young attorney who filed the lawsuit in federal court in San Jose, California, in 1973.

Upon learning of the pending lawsuit, the fire department's response was to isolate us in a small, windowless room at the training center. They provided us with a few books on the equipment, expecting us to pass the exam after only a few weeks of cramming. We saw this as another form of punishment—a deliberate attempt to set us up for failure. When we voiced our concerns about the inadequate conditions, the training officer dismissed them, insisting we should be grateful for the opportunity to retake the test and become full-time firefighters.

Fortunately, filing the lawsuit halted the fire department's efforts to terminate us, raising questions about their obligations to the EEA program and putting government funding at risk. Oddly, as Jerry and I sat in the small training classroom feeling ostracized, I reflected on my experience while attending protests of the Angela Davis trial in 1971/1972 in San Jose. I sat with Angela Davis's mother and sister on the steps of the federal courthouse on North First Street. As I sat with the family, I tried to console them and let them know that the small group of protesters believed Angela was innocent. They wanted the world to know about the injustice. Angela Davis was imprisoned in San Jose, California, from October 13, 1971, to February 23, 1972. She was held in the Santa Clara County jail awaiting trial on charges related to her alleged involvement in a courtroom shoot-out in Marin County, California. Davis was ultimately acquitted of all charges in 1972.[1] By no means were Jerry and I in danger of being imprisoned, like Angela Davis, but the treatment we had to endure from the white firefighter officers was unjust and harmed our relationship with the other firefighters.

Throughout this ordeal, I leaned on the support of Linda, my mother, and my grandmother, who believed in me and encouraged me to keep going. My grandmother passed away in 1973, but before she died, I had a chance to spend two weeks with her, talking about life events and my future. Granny could barely speak; she had suffered a stroke and was home recovering. I drove her around town and spent hours discussing our family; Granny would write messages and questions on a notepad. She believed in my decision to become a firefighter and saw it as a way for me to prosper.

In 1974, less than a year after the lawsuit was filed, the City of San Jose agreed to settle the case. As part of the settlement, the court required the San Jose Fire Department to hire professional test developers to create culturally sensitive, unbiased exams for all future hires. Additionally, the

1. James, *Angela Y. Davis.*

department was mandated to revise the physical test, ensuring that it was free from cultural bias and aligned with the actual training provided.

The fire department offered us full-time positions, covered our attorney fees, and allowed us to select our preferred fire stations. While we did not receive any monetary compensation, we had achieved the right to pursue our careers without the stigma of failure. Although Jerry aspired to a settlement of one million dollars, our attorney advised against seeking financial compensation and encouraged us to accept the settlement instead. Distrustful of the legal system, I relied on my gut and accepted the settlement for the sake of my family's well-being, a decision Jerry reluctantly supported. However, in our focus on the immediate outcome, we failed to consider the long-term implications. The time spent participating as a trainee and the time fighting for changes in the testing process was not factored into the calculation of our retirement benefits. We were unaware of the complexities surrounding the fire department's retirement system.

As permanent firefighters, we purchased homes in San Jose, establishing our families and becoming integral members of the city's Black middle class. I lived in my home until 1997, raising my daughters there throughout their adolescence. Our lawsuit earned us the admiration of the Black community, and we were celebrated as heroes, akin to the respect afforded to John Carlos and Tommie Smith for their courageous protest at the 1968 Olympics. Embracing this recognition, I quickly became an active member of the Black community and emerged as a leader among various social justice organizations, committed to advocating for equity and opportunity for all.

Chapter 4

You Have to Kill Me First

IN THIS CHAPTER, TRUSTY recounts a critical turning point in the formation of the Santa Clara County Black Firefighters Association (SCCBFA). Against the backdrop of a turbulent era of social justice movements, including the rise of Black organizations and the fight for civil rights, Trusty and his fellow firefighters found themselves not only battling systemic racism within the fire service but also facing internal resistance from those who doubted their commitment to change. The chapter details a pivotal organizing meeting that quickly escalated into a life-threatening confrontation, revealing the high stakes of their efforts and the courage required to fight both personal and institutional injustice.

Employment discrimination was a significant hurdle for women and people of color, and by the late 1960s, many social justice organizations began addressing the disparities in hiring and promotions. The fire service, like many other institutions, was slow to change, but the need for diversity and representation within fire departments became clear. Representation mattered—it shaped how minorities were perceived and emphasized their contributions to the community. The idea of equity gained momentum as people began demanding fairness and impartiality in employment and access to opportunity for all.

The International Association of Black Professional Fire Fighters (IABPFF) was founded in response to these inequalities in 1969. Created by African

American firefighters frustrated with the discriminatory practices within their departments, the IABPFF became a collective voice, advocating for diversity, equality, and justice within fire departments. The organization's scope expanded beyond the United States, including members from Africa and the Caribbean. Its founders—Chief James B. Nelson, Captain Earl Bakerville, Lieutenant Clayton Barnes, and others—held conferences and used public speaking and media to highlight the systemic challenges facing Black firefighters.[1]

I was always a voracious reader, deeply engaged in African and African American history. I read W. E. B. Du Bois, Frederick Douglass, James Baldwin, Martin Luther King Jr., Malcolm X, Fidel Castro, and Nelson Mandela. And I closely followed the events in Africa, particularly around apartheid and the struggles for independence. Living at Still Point and during my years as a firefighter trainee, I read constantly.

The African liberation movements of the 1960s and 1970s deeply shaped my approach to leadership. These movements resonated with me because the fight for independence in African nations paralleled the civil rights struggle and the pursuit of empowerment in the United States. I viewed myself as part of a larger Pan-African community, drawing strength from the shared experiences of countries fighting against colonialism, racism, and economic exploitation.

As a newly hired Black firefighter trainee, I quickly became fascinated by the rise of Black firefighter organizations across the country. The IABPFF was gaining momentum, and Los Angeles had already set the stage with the Stentorians in 1954, a pioneering group of Black firefighters fighting for their rights. San Francisco followed suit in 1969 with the Vulcan Society, standing up against the ongoing discrimination their Black firefighters faced. These organizations confirmed what I knew—we needed a chapter in Santa Clara County to protect ourselves.

In January 1973, Russell Hayden organized a meeting at Trotters Inn in Los Altos, gathering ten Black firefighters from across the county. These men represented Los Altos (Russell Hayden), Palo Alto (Ken Moore, Dennis Wright, and Cleveland Kennard), San Jose (Dudley Bynoe and Jerry Williams), Santa Clara County Central Fire Department (Angelo Chancellor), Mountain View (Ivy Chretien and Elmore Scott), and the City of Santa Clara (Brooker Moore). Jerry and I were the only trainees; the rest were full-time employees. Our mission was clear: to shield Black firefighters

1. Wikipedia, "International Association."

from the blatant racism we faced daily and to recruit more Black firefighters into the profession of firefighting.

From the very start, our new organization, the Santa Clara County Black Firefighters Association (SCCBFA), encountered internal friction. During one of our early organizing meetings, I made it clear we needed to confront the racism ingrained in the fire service. Jerry and I had already taken legal action against the City of San Jose for its racially biased testing practices, and I believed this case could be the leverage needed to launch our association. We had identified a social problem and an institutional failure that needed to be corrected. But not everyone agreed. One firefighter tried to dismiss me, claiming I had no say because I was still a trainee. He looked me in the eye and said, "You're not even a firefighter."

My response was immediate: "Fuck you. You wouldn't even be here if it weren't for me."

I make no apologies for my language. It was my truth, and the moment called for nothing less.

Things escalated fast. The firefighter stormed out, only to return minutes later with a rifle in hand. We were crammed in a small studio apartment with only one exit, and panic set in immediately. Jerry dove under the bed while everyone else pressed themselves against the walls, trying to get as far from the gunman as possible. Then, amid the chaos, Angelo Chancellor, one of our founding members, stepped forward. He stood between me and the man with the gun and said calmly, "You'll have to kill me first if you want to kill Trust."

At that moment, everyone froze in the room. Angelo's words were powerful and disarmed the situation. The firefighter, visibly shaking, slowly backed out of the apartment and never returned to another SCCBFA meeting. That was the moment our group's purpose became solidified. From then on, the SCCBFA wasn't just a group of Black firefighters trying to survive within a racist system. We became a collective force, determined to change the system itself. We were tested that night—both literally and figuratively—and we stood our ground.

Chapter 5

Level of Service

"LEVEL OF SERVICE" PORTRAYS Dudley Bynoe's experiences at Station 16, emphasizing the community challenges within the San Jose Fire Department. In his early days as a full-time firefighter, Dudley deliberately chose to work in East San Jose, a predominantly Black and brown community, where he hoped to improve the service and treatment the residents received from emergency responders. Throughout his time at Station 16, he faced blatant racism from his fellow firefighters, who often showed a lack of respect for the diverse community they served. He reflects on the insidious nature of the discrimination, which was not only exhibited in the actions of white firefighters but also embedded in the training and attitudes toward people of color. The chapter also delves into Trusty's personal growth as he learns to navigate the toxic environment of his workplace, finding solidarity and respect through his actions and defiance against systemic injustice. His encounters with firefighters, community members, and even law enforcement deepen his understanding of the intersection between race, service, and social responsibility in his profession. The chapter closes with a reflection on the emotional and psychological toll of these experiences, illustrating how they shaped not only his career but also his sense of justice and advocacy for change.

My first decision as a full-time firefighter was to choose the fire station to which I wanted to be assigned. We lived in a duplex on Malabar Drive in

East San Jose, just minutes from several fire stations. During my time as a firefighter trainee at various stations in San Jose, I noticed a stark contrast in the level of service and compassion provided to Black and brown communities in the East Side compared to the predominantly white communities on the west and south sides. For this reason, I chose to work in East San Jose, to bring a sense of altruism to the community and improve the level of service to a neglected area. My first choice was to be assigned to Station 16 on the C shift. Booker Law, the first Black full-time firefighter hired by the San Jose Fire Department, worked at Station 16 but on the A shift. Booker had a politically astute captain, Joe Paradiso, who made it clear that no one should mistreat Booker, allowing him to avoid the blatant racism and disrespect that I had to endure. However, as I spent more time with Booker and gained a deeper understanding of his background, I came to respect his knowledge and the strategies he employed to navigate anti-Black racism.

Station 16 served a working-class neighborhood that included African Americans, Mexican Americans, Asian Americans, and a few white families. Situated at the intersection of King and Cunningham, it was the second busiest fire station in San Jose. The busiest, Station 8, served both downtown and east-side communities, operating as a single-engine company that frequently collaborated with other stations, which resulted in a much higher volume of rescue calls. Station 16, however, was classified as a two-piece engine company comprised of both an engine and a truck company. Engine 16 was the second busiest engine in the city, while Truck 16 ranked as the busiest truck, specializing in rescue operations, ventilation, and salvage efforts.

Engine companies were tasked with directly attacking fires and providing medical services, while truck companies handled rescue operations. These included entering burning buildings to save trapped victims, responding to vehicle accidents, and addressing other emergencies where people were entrapped. Firefighters, early in their careers, were eager to work at Station 16 because its high volume of calls provided unparalleled exposure to all aspects of the fire service The East San Jose area experienced the most structure fires, vehicle accidents, and medical emergencies, such as heart attacks, suicides, and drug overdoses, giving firefighters extensive hands-on experience that was not as readily available at other stations throughout the city.

Low-income residential areas faced significant challenges, including limited access to education, employment, adequate housing, and equitable services from city agencies. At Station 16, the majority of firefighters and officers were white males, with one Mexican firefighter who often aligned himself with his white colleagues. Many of these white firefighters were eager to work at Station 16, drawn by the thrill of responding to emergencies such as fires, shootings, drug overdoses, vehicle rescues, and homicides. However, while they enjoyed the adrenaline rush of the job, I observed that they frequently harbored negative attitudes toward the very communities they were meant to serve, showing a lack of empathy and respect necessary for effective community engagement.

As a result, Station 16 frequently failed to live up to the San Jose Fire Department's mission of "Courtesy and Service." When white firefighters entered residents' homes, their behavior was often authoritarian and dismissive. They would verbally and physically disregard the residents' property, sometimes making disparaging remarks about the condition of their homes.

I observed that these firefighters frequently discarded residents' belongings without care, showing little regard for the value or significance of the item to the families. According to the fire department's rules and regulations, firefighters were required to ensure that a fire was fully extinguished before beginning overhaul operations, which included removing walls and ceilings. They were also instructed to carefully assess the home and make efforts to protect personal property such as furniture, photographs, jewelry, and other valuable items.

KNOW YOUR COMMUNITY: HISTORY OF EAST SAN JOSE

Having experienced the vibrancy of East San Jose and the opportunity to meet a few of their respected leaders, I understood that this community was seldom discussed positively, and its rich history remained largely undocumented. Many of the white firefighters appeared unaware of the communities' cultural diversity, often treating the residents as if they were less deserving of respect and consideration as human beings.

Before 1959, much of East San Jose was farmland extending into the eastern foothills, primarily inhabited by migrant agricultural workers. These workers lived in barrios lacking basic amenities like sewers, sidewalks, and streetlights. Alongside them, a small number of Black residents, as well as some Asians and whites, also settled in the East Side, drawn to the availability of low-cost housing. White property owners would rent to this diverse group of working-class people, subtly reinforcing the perception that Santa Clara County was segregated. Meanwhile, the San Jose's West Side remained white.

I often saw Cesar Chavez, the cofounder of the National Farm Workers Association and a powerful advocate for farm workers' rights, on television. He was a prominent figure in the well-known East Side neighborhood known locally as Sal Si Puedes, or "Get Out if You Can." I admired his calm, reflective demeanor and his ability to connect with his community. During a local news program, when asked about his dedication to nonviolence, he referenced his relationship with Martin Luther King Jr., which instantly piqued my attention.

The Chicano Movement significantly shaped life in East San Jose during the 1960s and 1970s. Education activists protested against local schools, such as the one on King Road. Ernestina Garcia, who founded El Comité Pro-Estudiantil, led a grassroots movement of Mexican parents opposing the school's policy of penalizing Mexican American children for speaking Spanish. Similarly, Sofia Mendoza organized junior high students, parents, teachers, and community members in one of San Jose's first Chicana/o student walkouts. She also fought against police brutality targeting Latino youth. Both women conducted their protests within our first-in area.[1]

Our Lady of Guadalupe Church was the heart of the Latino community, serving not only as a place of worship but also as a center for community support through holiday festivals and weddings. It was also a frequent meeting place for community activists.

HISTORY OF BLACK LEADERS IN SAN JOSE

When Linda and I moved to San Jose, we rented a duplex from Clyde and Ola Ribbs, a family with deep historical roots in East San Jose. The Ribbs family owned one of the first Black-owned businesses in the city. Clyde Ribbs worked as a janitor, owned a shoeshine stand, and served as a private chauffeur before purchasing Jones Transfer, a courier company that started with just one truck and a shoe stand at Second and San Fernando Street. His wife, Ola, became an active community leader, serving as a member of the Garden City Women's Club and the secretary of the local NAACP. She also represented the Order of the Eastern Star on the Council of Civic Unity.

---

1. The "first-in" area encompasses the area where, if there were a fire, the company would be the ones expected to arrive first.

Clyde's brother, Henry Ribbs, began his career as an apprentice to Theodore T. Moss, San Jose's first African American plumber. Henry later became a licensed plumber himself and, in 1927, founded Ribbs Plumbing, Heating, and Sheet Metal Company, which became the first business of its kind owned by an African American west of the Mississippi River.[2] After joining the plumber's union, Henry worked to help other African Americans gain membership as well. He built several homes in East San Jose, and in 1960, the street between Foss Avenue and Jackson Avenue was named Ribbs Lane in his honor.

One of the most remarkable members of the Ribbs family I had the pleasure of meeting was Willy T. Ribbs, Henry's grandson. Willy made his mark in motorsports, starting as a rookie driver in the English Formula Ford Championship, where he won six out of eleven races. In 1986, he became the first African American to drive a Formula One car, and in 1991, he made history again by becoming the first African American to qualify for the Indianapolis 500. Throughout my journey, I have met many influential leaders and unsung heroes, and I feel honored to have witnessed the accomplishments of these Latinos and African Americans during their time.

The white firefighters serving our first-in neighborhood were either unaware or in denial about the systemic racism affecting people of color. They failed to recognize that guns and drugs were intentionally funneled into these communities, designed to undermine hopes and opportunities. What the community needed wasn't just essential services but confident, culturally aware police and fire department personnel who understood the challenges and could respond with respect and care. These communities deserved not only safety but equitable, thoughtful services that uplifted rather than alienated them.

An incident occurred near Station 16 where a San Jose police officer killed a Black man. The victim heard a commotion in his backyard and went outside with a shotgun to protect his home from who he thought may be intruders. The police officers, while chasing a low-level drug dealer through his backyard, shot and killed the Black homeowner. Station 16 responded to this EMS call to provide necessary medical care. After the incident, some of the police officers involved came to my station for coffee and rest. Typically, the conversation centers around what happened and what you may have heard after a high-stress event. The officers sitting at the table were bragging about killing the Black man. There was a Black officer

2. Inda, "East Side Revelations."

in the midst of the conversation. He stated that "it was a good shoot." I took it that the Black officer was indicating that killing the Black man was the right thing to do.

I confronted the Black officer and asked him to step away with me to the apparatus floor. Once we were out of earshot, I inquired why he felt the killing was justified. I reenacted the scene, emphasizing that the Black man involved was merely a community resident trying to protect his property while the police invaded his backyard without identifying themselves or assessing the situation. The officer responded bluntly, saying it was none of my business and that he didn't owe me an explanation. I told him I never wanted to see him in the station again.

He shouted back, "You are not the captain and have no right to make such a demand." I replied, as I typically did in heated moments, "Mother-fucker, if you don't like it, take your gun off, and we can settle this now." After that, the officer left and never returned to Station 16 during my shift again.

THE PREVALENT DISRESPECT

The same contempt shown toward me by many of the white firefighters at Station 16 was expressed to people of the East Side community. During emergency calls, I was not given an assignment. For example, when we arrived at an auto accident, the white firefighters would grab all the rescue tools and head to their assignment, leaving nothing for me to do but stand by and watch. As a new firefighter, I should have been assigned to shadow a senior firefighter. The senior firefighter would coach me as I learned to use the tools and learned the process to follow regarding the specific incident. Firefighters work as a team and learn to function under pressure from the team's experiences. The station captain's role was to see that I was provided these opportunities and not left out and demeaned. It appeared that the captain decided that losing their white supremacy status, which preserved existing power structures and denied others equal rights, was more important.

Finally, one white firefighter named Sam Francisco dared to go against his peers and questioned them about excluding me from the call. He said, "How can Dudley learn how to react in an emergency if he is not allowed to participate in the process?" It was clear to him that if I had been a white rookie, they would have provided me with more opportunities to learn the skills needed to do my job effectively. Slowly, the captain started to include me in calls and station duties.

Some of the most annoying tactics and attitudes used toward me included leaving the day room as I entered and voting to change the TV station while I was watching a program. I quickly realized that I needed a sanctuary from the toxic atmosphere of Station 16. Often, I would stand outside the fire station to escape the hostility from my white coworkers. Located on a busy street that served as one of the major thoroughfares of the East Side, Station 16 attracted the attention of individuals from the neighborhood and surrounding areas. When people drove by and saw me standing near the flagpole in my uniform, it didn't take long for them to recognize me as a firefighter. Soon, they began waving, honking their horns, shouting greetings, or stopping to ask questions. Engaging with young people and friendly neighbors helped me cope with the isolation and animosity I felt from my colleagues. Being visible to the community also provided them with a sense of security; they knew someone was looking out for them. The residents, both young and old, affectionately nicknamed me "The Fireman."

One day, as I stood outside Station 16 near the flagpole, the captain came out of his office, ostensibly to check on me. He lingered for a short while, observing the traffic. However, instead of initiating a casual conversation or seeking to understand me better, he chose to comment on the dents he noticed on many cars in the neighborhood, counting them as if they were points of ridicule. I sensed that he expected me to engage with him, but I remained silent. His remarks indicated that he had no genuine concern for me or the community. Once again, I witnessed his assertion of superiority as he pointed out something he deemed negative, suggesting that the people in this neighborhood were reckless and unfit drivers. This particular captain later became a training officer and instructed all recruits to avoid interactions with me.

A fire department's main priority was to respond to emergency calls. When a company was not responding to emergency incidents, they were responsible for other things associated with the community and the station. Station personnel were responsible for fire safety inspections of all multi-family residential and commercial properties within their first-in area. There were also requirements to test and inspect fire hydrants and sprinkler systems, provide fire safety demonstrations, and continuously educate the crew on firefighting prevention—training the team on effective firefighting techniques, fire prevention strategies, rescue operations, and emergency medical procedures. When we were not doing those things, everyone could do their own thing within the station, such as watch TV, read books, lift weights, or play sports. Without exception, it was during this time many firefighters would isolate, humiliate, and aggravate me.

After an ordinary, routine neighborhood call, we returned to the station to clean up the trucks. One of the white firefighters loudly said, "I am tired of going on calls with those people." When I heard this statement, the hair on the back of my neck bristled; I had enough. I asked sarcastically, "What people are you talking about?" He responded, "Your people!" I immediately turned the six-foot-long, two-hundred-pound dining room table on him, pinning him to the back wall. It took several crew members to stop me. The same captain who stood in front of Station 16 with me counting dents in residence cars was the person who stopped me from wanting to kill the fool who had brazenly disrespected Black and brown people, my people.

Another disturbing situation occurred when an elderly African American man I knew from the neighborhood had a heart attack. As soon as the Station 16 crew arrived, we started CPR. Then the ambulance arrived with paramedics, and the elder was put on a gurney. I assisted the paramedics in the ambulance by providing CPR. The paramedics performed an electric shock procedure, and the elder's heart started beating. While on the way to the hospital, one of the paramedics in communications with the emergency room stated, "This is a seventy-plus-year-old Black man in atrial fibrillation, and he will not make it." When I heard this statement, I was concerned that the hospital might not do everything to save the older Black man because it appeared the paramedics had already given up on him. Unfortunately, he did not make it. I wanted to file a complaint against the paramedics and the hospital, but there was not enough definitive evidence that they had failed to provide the proper level of service. Without the possibility of recourse, that incident stayed on my mind for several months.

One of the most humiliating situations I endured occurred during my first annual advanced first aid training class at the fire station, led by an outside consulting group. This particular session focused on treating gunshot wounds using cadavers of young Black men with bullet holes in their heads, bodies, and elsewhere. The use of mannequins designed as corpses had persisted for several years. I felt the value of Black life was not only disrespected but also reduced to a stereotype. Witnessing this depiction of Black men ignited a profound anger within me; I lost control and expressed my outrage using language that was both forceful and blasphemous, reflecting the gravity of the situation. I approached the station captain, the consultants, and several fire administration officers to protest the use of these types of cadavers. My bold stand prompted immediate change; they ceased using only Black cadavers for training. Since EMS training falls under county jurisdiction, my protest reverberated throughout all Santa Clara County fire departments. Quickly, the country reassessed its use of Black cadavers in training and started using cadavers (mannequins) that represented other racial groups.[3]

This incident brought back haunting memories of the Watts riots in the summer of 1965. I had served in the United States Army in an infantry brigade at Fort Ord, California, predominantly made up of young Black men. I vividly recall the headline in the *Monterey Herald* that read, "Thirty-Five Negros Were Killed Today and One American." The fury among my fellow Black soldiers and me was palpable. I had just left the army months before my brigade was deployed to Vietnam in November 1965, where many were tragically killed. My friends died in Vietnam, yet they were never truly regarded as Americans. The emotional weight of these experiences—of humiliation, anger, and grief—remains deeply etched in my memory.

MY CAREER CHANGE ON CHRISTMAS DAY, 1974

On Christmas morning, 1974, we got a call for a first-alarm structure fire at a home that Station 16 firefighters knew well. It was a call to the home of a poor white family in the neighborhood. When we arrived, the front of the house was in flames. I was assigned to Truck 16; my job was to search and rescue any trapped victims. Working as a team, a white firefighter and I determined the best way to enter the structure was through a bedroom window in the back. The white firefighter entered first. As I prepared to enter through the window, the white firefighter, for some reason, decided to exit and pushed me backward as he left the building. I decided to enter the residence alone. I felt it was necessary to try to rescue anyone still living.

The bedroom was hot, and the smoke was so thick that I could not see my hand in front of my face. I lowered to my stomach and began rescue procedures. It was like searching a room with your eyes blindfolded. We were taught that when searching, you must search under beds, in closets, and corners because panicking would cause a person or child to cover and

---

3. Many fire departments nationwide, and all fire departments in California, made this change.

hide. I used the axe to increase my reach. I recovered the first body within seconds. It appeared to be a small child. I was able to hand the victim off to other members of my crew outside the structure. Several times, I went into the bedrooms and found a total of five young children in fatal condition due to smoke inhalation. This incident affected me psychologically and emotionally at home and at work for many years.[4]

That morning, I went home, Christmas Day, to see my daughters, Nicola and Traci, who were seven and eight years old, but instead was greeted by the press, the San Jose *Mercury*, and other local TV stations. In 1974, professional firefighters were expected to maintain a macho image. The model of all-white fire departments throughout the country was to be community heroes and show no fear or emotions. Based on my prior history with the San Jose Fire Department, I had to show strength and present a strong front. In private, I was depressed, unable to play with my daughters or enjoy the holidays.

None of the fire department officers on site commented or disciplined the firefighter who left me alone that Christmas Day. Years later, the white firefighter was promoted to the position of captain. Every time he saw me, he hung his head. We knew his actual value. However, my crew became more respectful of my ability to fight fires. As I encountered two- and three-alarm fires with other fire station firefighters, I gained respect as a good firefighter throughout the department. Even after demonstrating my skills of being a competent firefighter, white firefighters did not change their attitude toward my rhetoric or their white supremacist actions toward other Black firefighters and the Black and brown community.

Station 16's C shift captains assessed my annual performance evaluations for years as merely average. Years later, I determined I should have challenged the evaluations because other less able firefighters were evaluated above average. I had never cared about grades and felt passing was acceptable because of the horrific educational experiences I endured as a child. White and Black firefighters acknowledged me as an excellent firefighter, speaker, and activist, attributes that were meaningful to me as I learned more about the inequitable ways people got rewarded on their evaluations. Lesson learned: I challenged every time anyone wanted to grade me as merely average for anything.

---

4. The event was reported on in the San Jose *Mercury News* on December 25, 1974.

Chapter 6

The Multidimensional Chess Player

CHAPTER 6 FOCUSES ON a pivotal period in the growth and development of the SCCBFA, reflecting both the personal journey of Trusty and the broader fight for racial equity in the firefighting profession. Stepping into the role of SCCBFA's second president, Trusty worked tirelessly to establish a stable foundation for the association, including securing a permanent meeting space and prioritizing recruitment for Black firefighters. The chapter also highlights the author's commitment to empowering future generations of Black firefighters, inspired by the civil rights movements of the 1960s and the activism of figures like Tommie Smith and John Carlos.

The SCCBFA's growth is detailed, showing how strategic alliances—such as the one with Angelo Chancellor—helped shape its mission. The chapter also discusses the critical partnership with the International Association of Black Professional Firefighters (IABPFF), which provides resources for recruitment, training, and advocacy. These efforts led to significant success in getting Black firefighters hired, notably influencing the appointment of Robert Osby as San Jose's first Black fire chief in 1985.

Trusty expresses his transformation from a militant advocate for Black firefighters to a skilled political strategist, a leader determined to ensure Black firefighters were represented within the union and given equal opportunities for advancement.

The SCCBFA went through various stages of growth, from initial turbulence to eventually forming a strong, united association. When I became a full-time firefighter, I was elected as the second president of the SCCBFA, succeeding Russell Hayden. I brought a more passionate and militant perspective to the group, determined to advocate for Black firefighters and confront systemic racism. One of my priorities was securing a permanent meeting place for the SCCBFA, rather than rotating between members' homes or fire stations. Black firefighters needed a consistent space to gather, discuss strategies, and address grievances for eight fire departments across Santa Clara County. Our primary purpose was to recruit and prepare more Black candidates for fire department testing. The Bynoe-Williams lawsuit had challenged the testing to become more job-related, opening up new opportunities. As president, my approach was often militant, shaped by the persistent anti-Black racism I faced as an EEA trainee and firefighter at Station 16. Luckily, I had confidants who helped me channel my anger productively. One of my key allies was Angelo Chancellor, a calm, highly educated, and culturally astute Black man from Oakland. His levelheadedness was invaluable during my tenure as president, as he served as secretary on the SCCBFA Executive Board. Together, we worked to establish stronger ties with Black community organizations and elevate the SCCBFA as a legitimate force in San Jose.

In 1974, I approached Bob Stroughter, director of the Mayfair Neighborhood Center, to request space for SCCBFA's meetings and recruitment classes aimed at young Black men aspiring to become firefighters. Stroughter generously gave us a room for our meetings and recruitment efforts, recognizing the importance of what we were trying to achieve. We also organized community service initiatives such as food drives, book drives, and healthcare programs, including screenings for high blood pressure and heart disease and distributing free smoke detectors to elderly residents.

The 1968 Olympic medalists and San Jose State University students Tommie Smith and John Carlos raised their fists at the Mexico City Olympics in a powerful stand against white supremacy. This act of resistance resonated deeply within Black communities, instilling pride and inspiring action. Our victory in the court case against the city's discriminatory testing process had a similar effect locally, elevating us as militant figures within the community. This recognition helped me connect with other Black leaders and broaden our influence.

Later that year, the SCCBFA joined the IABPFF, a network of chapters spanning the United States, Africa, and the Caribbean. Our regional branch, known as the Southwest Region of the IABPFF, included seven states: Nevada, California, Arizona, Hawaii, Utah, Colorado, and New Mexico. We partnered with the Oakland chapter of the IABPFF, which significantly bolstered our recruitment efforts by providing resources like written test samples, physical agility requirements, and oral board practices for interview preparation. The first class to go through our program produced six or seven new hires who passed the San Jose Fire Department's exam on their first try.

The SCCBFA's recruitment classes were pivotal in getting Black firefighters hired, not just in San Jose but also in Milpitas, Santa Clara, Sunnyvale, Palo Alto, Mountain View, and Menlo Park. Over the course of twenty years, hundreds of our firefighter recruits rose to prominent positions, from engineers to fire chiefs. Notably, SCCBFA played a crucial role in the hiring of San Jose's first Black fire chief, Robert Osby, in 1985.

As the SCCBFA grew, it became a powerful political voice in Santa Clara County. Under my leadership, the association worked closely with Black community organizations such as the NAACP, Urban League, and the A. Philip Randolph Institute, among others. We also prioritized supporting Black-owned businesses, and in return, these businesses backed our fundraising events, which included youth camps, senior citizen care, and annual community fundraising dances.

However, the need for advocacy against racist action was always present. A training academy incident occurred when a Black probationary firefighter came to me after being unfairly terminated. I consulted with another Black probationary firefighter, Lacy Atkinson, and confirmed that this was a case of racial discrimination. The white training officers disliked the terminated firefighter's attitude, but it was clear that race played a role in that decision. Although the firefighter chose not to follow my advice and ultimately lost his job, this incident solidified my relationship with Atkinson, who became one of my strongest supporters and an advocate for justice within the department.

The racist incident at the training center became another catalyst for the SCCBFA to push for change. When firefighter recruits transitioned to probationary firefighters, they were assigned to the training academy for orientation. This orientation included an employee benefits package, a presentation by Human Resources, and an introduction to union representation.

With our growing political influence, SCCBFA leaders believed we had the right to present our organization's benefits at these orientations. To pursue this, I set up a meeting with Fire Chief Vince Clet—the department's first white fire chief—to recognize my deep concerns about the challenges Black firefighters were facing.

During our conversation, I requested that a SCCBFA representative be allowed to speak at the next orientation to inform recruits about our association. This request stemmed from troubling comments made to Black recruits by training officers, warning them to avoid me, "Dudley Bynoe." I had been labeled "bad news" and a troublemaker, with white officers implying that associating with me could harm their careers.

After a series of heated discussions, Clet eventually agreed to allow all firefighter associations to present their mission, benefits, and guidelines during orientation. This opened the door for groups like the Los Bomberos, the Women Firefighter Association, the Asian Firefighters, and others to expand their outreach. During the mid-1970s to mid-1980s, probationary firefighters could be terminated if a training officer felt they didn't align with the white firefighters' cultural expectations. When I presented at Orientation Day, I emphasized that for just ten dollars a month, new firefighters could join the SCCBFA, gaining a cultural connection and the support that would guide them through their careers.

MY NEXT CHALLENGE: THE UNION LOCAL 873/230

My first introduction to Local 873/230, the firefighters' union, occurred when Jerry Williams and I challenged the entry-level written exam. One day, several union members showed up at the training center while Jerry and I were studying the civil service manual in preparation for the written exam. They asked why we were challenging the exam. After a brief conversation, we asked them what they wanted and why they were approaching trainees. They said their goal was to protect all firefighters and wanted to be aware if the testing process was going to change. We didn't trust their sincerity, especially since they didn't represent us as trainees, so we dismissed them.

When I became a permanent firefighter, members of Local 873/230 approached me again about joining the union. I chose to join because I believed in the union's role in securing employee benefits, improving working conditions, negotiating pay, and addressing the diverse needs of firefighters. It was common knowledge that many union members also held positions as fire department administration officers, and I recognized that Local 873/230 represented firefighters up to the rank of battalion chief.

In 1975, I began attending the monthly meetings of Local 873, which later changed its designation to Local 230 in the late 1980s. It quickly became apparent that I was the only Black firefighter participating in these meetings, a solitude that lasted for five long years. During this time, I immersed myself in understanding the Memorandum of Understanding (MOU)—the negotiated agreement between the firefighters' union and the City of San Jose—as well as the fire department rules and regulations and relevant federal and state laws. This knowledge not only empowered me but also opened doors to engage with other municipalities, fire departments, and their unions.

The union's effort to block progress and equity extended beyond union meetings. The union leaders portrayed negotiations as benefiting all members, but the truth was that decisions were being made long before the members knew what was on the table. Their focus was on maintaining their power and privilege, not on ensuring that all firefighters, particularly Black firefighters, were fairly represented. It was no secret that the union leadership had padded their salaries—earning not just a firefighter's pay but also a union officer's salary. This gave them a financial incentive to keep their positions and resist any efforts to shake things up.

I knew that I had the intellectual aptitude, beliefs, and vocabulary to advocate for Black firefighters mistreated by white firefighters. Over time, I saw that Black firefighters' grievances were often ignored. One story that stuck with me was about the first Black firefighter in San Jose, who had been promoted to fire engineer but wasn't allowed to operate the fire engine. At the time, a Class B license was required to drive emergency vehicles over twenty-six thousand pounds. Driving the fire engine, which carried water and hoses, was essential. That Black fire engineer confided in me about his situation but was afraid to complain, fearing retaliation. I took it upon myself to confront his white captain about the issue. After our conversation, the captain allowed him to drive all the appropriate vehicles. This victory boosted my reputation as a strong advocate for Black firefighters and sent a message: Black firefighters had a voice, and we weren't afraid to use it.

As a result of my advocacy, Black firefighters throughout Santa Clara County began coming to me, sharing their stories of discrimination, abuse, and threats of discipline. While I could resolve most of these issues at a lower level, some required me to use political leverage to ensure fair treatment from city officials. But despite all this, I refused to be silenced. Every time I attended a meeting and was dismissed or ignored, it only strengthened my resolve. It became clear that the leadership feared change. They feared me and what would happen if Black firefighters gained equity. And that's exactly why I had to keep fighting, even when it felt like I was up against an immovable force. Yet I thought it was apropos, it felt like a game of chess, and I was the "Multidimensional Chess Player."

The San Jose Fire Department was the largest in Santa Clara County, and I knew I had to immerse myself in the political workings of Local 873/230. The union had significant influence over the city's election process, fundraising for the mayor, city council, district attorneys, county supervisors, and state representatives. I volunteered at union-sponsored events to better understand their operations and build my political presence.

Over time, I realized that many Black union members were paying substantial dues but didn't benefit much from the union's power. This realization motivated me to push for Black firefighters to ascend to leadership positions. If we were valuable contributors, both in numbers and financial support, we could play a bigger role in decision-making. Unfortunately, many Black firefighters distrusted the union and were reluctant to take on that challenge. As I grew politically, I decided it was time to pursue a spot on the executive board of Local 873/230. I attended union meetings to learn how the good-ole-boy network operated. The executive board, made up of close friends and neighbors, ran the organization like a social club. The president and his inner circle made decisions and dictated resolutions that would later be presented to the membership for a vote.

During union meetings from the mid-1970s to the mid-1980s, white members often made microaggressive, racist remarks, calling Black men "boys," saying people of color didn't belong or that we should leave our cultural baggage at the door. Sometimes, they ignored anything said by people of color. While they professed to support civil rights and fairness, they maintained their white supremacy–based network and were not honest brokers of equity. When confronted with these challenges, I used language that was direct and inflammatory. If I believed a white firefighter was an anti-Black racist, I called him a "white racist motherfucker," regardless of his position—whether union president, mayor, or city manager.

White firefighters occasionally invited a Black firefighter to union meetings to represent their viewpoint, often to undermine my ideas. But if a Black firefighter betrayed our community, I used the same language towards him, but he was a "Black racist motherfucker." It didn't matter whether you were Black or white—if you humiliated or disrespected me, you became my enemy, requiring a language that expressed a level of disgust that alarmed most men.

My passion stemmed from years of being treated as an "ugly Black man," a label others used to describe me. I never felt ugly; I reclaimed that label and turned it into a tool for change. I found that the "Ugly Black Man" resonated with others and became a powerful weapon for influencing policy. If my accusations had been false, I wouldn't have been as effective as I was.

I worked with several union executive board members across different fire stations, learning their personalities, strengths, cowardice, and attitudes toward Black people. After union meetings, members would head next door to the union-owned bar for drinks. Occasionally, I would go to observe, knowing that after a few drinks, some of the white firefighters, emboldened by alcohol, might reveal their true feelings.

The first Black fire chief, Robert Osby, hired in 1985, told me in 2022 that when the city manager offered him the position, a key reason was to calm me down and address problems with Black firefighters. When Chief Osby met with his command staff and the union president, the first question they asked was, "What are you going to do about Dudley Bynoe?"

One of many moves to improve and engage the
community: high blood pressure screening.

Chapter 7

Effective but Too Ghetto

THIS CHAPTER DELVES INTO the pivotal moments of Trusty's leadership with the SCCBFA and his involvement in the IABPFF. It recounts the challenges he faced combating systemic racism within the fire service and among his peers, where solidarity often clashed with internal divisions. Through pivotal incidents—like mobilizing against racial harassment in Milpitas and navigating tense union negotiations—Trusty learned hard lessons about leadership, resilience, and the cost of advocacy. The chapter also explores the personal toll of these struggles on the family and his own identity, underscoring the complexities of fighting for equity while grappling with betrayal and self-reflection. Above all, it reflects on the balance between militant activism and the need for strategic partnerships to achieve lasting change.

My experiences with the IABPFF and the Southwest Region empowered me and reinforced the urgent need to combat anti-Black racism. I could no longer tolerate the systemic white supremacist attitudes that were pervasive in the San Jose Fire Department. Despite my efforts to extend the influence of the SCCBFA throughout the county, white firefighters continued to bully, discourage, and undermine our initiatives to increase membership.

In 1977, a young Black firefighter from the Milpitas Fire Department was harassed and humiliated by a white union representative who smashed a cupcake in his face and spray-painted the words "Die Nigger" on his car. At that time, I was the president of the SCCBFA, and we were hosting a conference with all chapter presidents of the IABPFF. Upon learning of the incident, we mobilized over one hundred Black firefighters and engaged the press to address the situation at the Milpitas Fire Department Administration Office. Our collective response led to significant changes in Milpitas's hiring and promotional processes. Under Fire Chief Harwood's leadership, Milpitas hired more Black firefighters per capita than any other city in Santa Clara County. The recognition that followed this incident spurred further changes in hiring practices throughout the county and elevated the SCCBFA's power and prominence.

As the president of the SCCBFA, I became actively involved in the Southwest Region of the IABPFF. I believed that our strength lay in our numbers and that many white firefighters in leadership positions were tirelessly plotting to undermine our achievements. I strongly urged SCCBFA members to attend conferences and seminars organized by the Southwest Region, as these events fostered a sense of unity, empowerment, and camaraderie among us, all dedicated to protecting and recruiting new Black firefighters.

My approach to our mission was decidedly militant; I refused to be swayed by ego, politics, or appeasement. I insisted that we remain focused on recruitment and equity for all Black firefighters, regardless of rank. As some SCCBFA members ascended to leadership positions within the Southwest Region, it became clear that our influence was growing. Despite being a relatively new organization with fewer than fifty members, the SCCBFA consistently achieved higher attendance at conferences and seminars than larger, more established associations, such as the Stentorians from Los Angeles County and other firefighter associations from Los Angeles, Oakland, and San Francisco.

Through participation in these events, SCCBFA members gained valuable insights into the fire service, leadership techniques, and promotional skills by networking with Black firefighters from other cities and states. I formed strong friendships with several members of the Southwest Region by attending these regional organizational events. Notable individuals included Bob Demons and Joe Morrison from the San Francisco Black Firefighters Association; Bill Parkers, Herschel Clady, and Ollie Linson from the LA County Stentorians; Benny Scott, David Washinton, and Vergus Porter from the Clark County Black Firefighters Association in Nevada; and Frank Chetham from the Phoenix United Black Firefighters.

Additionally, I connected with hundreds of brothers and sisters throughout the region.

My interactions with the founding members and early members of the IABPFF were distinct; while they were traditionalists, I often took a more militant approach. Although we sometimes clashed respectfully, I deeply admired many of their leaders, such as David Floyd of the New York City Fire Department and Charlie Hendrix of the Philadelphia Fire Department. They were older and more experienced, and I valued their perspectives. David Floyd, the president of the IABPFF, and Ron Taylor, the vice president, would often listen to my ideas and reframe my statements to align with their conservative viewpoints.

Challenges were especially intense during meetings with the white-dominated International Association of Firefighters (IAFF). The organization was entrenched in complex processes, and its leadership was overwhelmingly controlled by white members. At those meetings, I knew I had to make my presence known, so I used my voice with force and authority to ensure I was recognized.

The San Jose Fire Department chief, Vince Clet, recognized my leadership and passion for the SCCBFA members. Over time, we developed a respectful relationship that allowed us to work together toward a cohesive alliance between white and Black firefighters. One of Clet's first olive branches was instituting the Rule of Ten, a rule proposed through California affirmative action laws to increase opportunities for people of color and women. The Rule of Ten worked like this: If the fire administration was going to hire one position off a promotional list, they could interview and consider the top ten on the promotional list. If they were going to hire two positions, they were able to interview and consider the top twelve on the promotional list. They did not have to hire straight down the list.

I wanted to focus on issues that I believed were legitimate and beneficial for Black firefighters. One significant concern resulted in the union's negotiation for the city to pay overtime at time and a half for any hours worked beyond regular shift hours, rather than the straight pay that was currently being provided. Firefighters who had to extend their shifts due to a fire or other incidents received only regular pay for the additional time worked. The union insisted that this pay structure was unfair and encouraged its members not to work overtime.

I felt that I could inspire a few Black firefighters to unite with white firefighters from various county and city unions to advocate for an improvement in overtime pay. I approached Fire Chief Clet and requested permission to address the overtime issues and concerns of Local 873/230, specifically targeting Black firefighters who typically worked overtime. Clet, representing the City of San Jose, authorized me to work on the union's proposal to increase overtime pay.

The negotiations for time and a half overtime pay also included discussions about minimum staffing, which referred to the number of personnel required to adequately staff all engine and truck companies daily within the city. Firefighters wishing to work overtime would sign up in advance to be considered for minimum staffing positions. To fill these roles, the fire department would hire back those who signed up. However, if there were not enough firefighters on the minimum staffing list, a mandatory call-back procedure would be implemented, meaning off-duty firefighters would receive phone calls to report to work. If they answered the call, they were required to come back to work; failure to report to the station after accepting the call caused the firefighter to be disciplined.

I now recognize that my perspective was limited and often shaped by my own biases. Leaders can be harmed when they lack a comprehensive understanding of how they are perceived by others, even those who are members of the culture. My goal was to engage with Black firefighters who frequently worked minimum staffing. My goal was to present a rationale that seemed important to me and that I had hoped was important to them. I believed that if Black firefighters supported Local 875/230's initiative for time and a half pay, the union would begin to respect them as fellow members, and I would gain recognition as a leader within both the union and the SCCBFA. If I could gain this respect for my leadership skills, Black firefighters throughout the department would gain a voice in their favor. Chief Clet trusted me to handle these encounters appropriately but warned of severe consequences if anything went wrong. As I left the chief's office, Dick Santos approached me and asked about my meeting with Clet. I shared my plan to garner support from Black firefighters for the time and a half negotiations. Dick Santos, one of my white union supporters and friend, cautioned me to be careful. He told me that some Black firefighters had recently expressed feelings of jealousy and vindictiveness towards me.

My first visit was to Station 5, where one of my friends worked a minimum staffing shift. I started explaining my reason for the visit to their station. My friend Roland Hooks and another firefighter, Jerome Riggins, were playing pool, so I felt confident that the debate between three Black men was safe. I explained to Roland that I supported the proposed time and a half resolution of Local 873/230. I felt this was a fair resolution and that Black firefighters needed to help get it passed if we expected the union to support us and that everyone would gain increased pay when the initiative passed. Suddenly, Jerome Riggins went into a tirade, called me an uppity Black nigger, and said I thought I was special because I had an open-door policy with Chief Clet. My response was equally nasty, "Fuck you, motherfucker . . ." Jerome left the station and returned to the pool room with a bayonet sticking through his pocket and resting on his pant leg. I immediately thought that he was going to kill me. I charged him with my briefcase. As we ran out of the pool room through the parking lot, the entire crew exited the station to stop the possibility of a deadly incident. Several reports were written. One report insinuated that the Blacks were going wild.

Even though I was warned that some Black firefighters were envious of my influence, I struggled to accept that there was a vindictive element among them, nor did I want to start distrusting my fellow Black firefighters. The betrayal was particularly hurtful; I had dedicated my entire career to advocating for the betterment of Black firefighters. Some Black firefighters were angry that I chose to address the issue of better pay for minimum staffing, believing that if Black firefighters were "stupid enough" to accept regular pay, they should face the consequences of their decision. Some of my friends were angry that I continued to put my reputation on the line for those who they believed were unworthy. Some Black firefighters were pleased that the fire department had a reason to take me down.

I received the maximum discipline, six months without pay, along with the firefighter who started the confrontation. I was also embarrassed because Chief Clet was the first white chief to provide open-door discussions. He recognized the Black firefighters' plight for equity in the fire service and the need to bridge the gap between Black and white firefighters. Chief Clet trusted me to be judicious. Confident that Riggins had started the incident and that I should not have been blamed for defending myself, I took my case to the Civil Service Commission, hoping for a better outcome. Unfortunately, the board of commissioners agreed with the City of San Jose. They determined that we were both to blame.

The Southwest Region of the IABPFF sent two chapter presidents, Robert Demmons from San Francisco and Chief John Wells from Vallejo, to support me. I hired an attorney, Harry Robinson, to represent me in the civil service hearing. Robinson suggested that I file charges against the other firefighter because he came after me with a weapon, threatening my life. However, true to my principles, I could not bring charges against a fellow Black firefighter; it wasn't something I was raised to do. Growing up in New York City and later Long Island, I was acutely aware of the devastating impact police records could have on young Black men. Even my experiences in California were replete with police profiling, harassment, and disrespect. How could I risk another Black man experiencing police brutality, losing his job, or destroying his family? Until this traumatic event, I thought the SCCBFA members were family; our families dined, partied, and regularly visited each other.

My family suffered both financially and emotionally during this turbulent time. Because I was always home, Linda and the girls' schedules changed significantly. I wanted to take control of everything at home, which led to an unhealthy level of anxiety for Linda and my daughters. They were accustomed to me being at work for twenty-four-hour shifts at least ten days a month, allowing them to establish their routine of hanging out together, preparing special dinners, and enjoying outings. Despite my efforts to manage my embarrassment and anger, nothing seemed to work. I ran long distances daily, meditated, and spent quality time with my daughters to navigate this soul-searching period. After a couple of weeks of enduring my depression, Linda told me that I needed space and time to cope with the outcome of the hearing. She was concerned about the negative impact my anger was having on our daughters, who couldn't understand my disposition.

Recognizing Linda and my daughters' need for respite, I flew to New York City to spend time with my mother. Like Granny, my mother loved me unconditionally and was aware of my quirky temperament. She encouraged me to relax and reflect on my actions toward Riggins. I cherished the time with my mother in New York City, feeling free from responsibilities and worries. It was the first time I entertained the thought of moving back to New York. However, Linda was not on board with this idea; she understood that my family would never accept her way of being—and she didn't want our daughters to grow up in that restrictive, conservative milieu.

The visit with my mother was one of my best vacations. My mother rented a car, and I drove her everywhere she wanted to go. We left home every morning for a new adventure; sometimes we shopped in the city, visited an amusement park, gambled at a casino, or went to the ocean, and several times, we ventured outside New York City. The first trip was to

Connecticut, where we visited family members. Another trip was to Richmond, Virginia, stopping on the way many times to enjoy the monuments, museums, and government buildings of Washington, DC. I eventually returned to San Jose with an improved attitude. I avoided SCCBFA meetings and fire department events and gave attention to my family.

Feeling rejuvenated and ready to embark on a new project, I took a closer look at my little community of East San Jose. Our house was situated in an area that had a cabana club that included a swimming pool, tennis courts, and a golf course. There were several schools nearby, and they all had basketball courts. One day, while playing a game of twenty-one with Jerry Williams, I noticed several young Black guys enter the court. They asked to play a game with us. Despite my apprehension—after all, they were teenagers, and Jerry and I were grown men—we welcomed them. This was my first encounter with Carl Lacey, Mitch Collins, and Greg Johnson. Jerry and I were stronger and larger but not necessarily more athletically talented; we used our size to take advantage and win the game.

Surprisingly, despite my aggressive tactics, they did not complain, nor did they give up. They were not afraid of our physicality or my outrageous vocabulary. They stood their ground, and we became friends for life. I was the designated godfather, and they were my comrades.

A couple of years earlier, during a union political meeting, I joined the Big Brother organization and was paired with Anthony Colman. Anthony was thirteen years old, a child raised by a single mother. He lived in East San Jose, a few streets from Station 16. Anthony visited me often at the fire station. He was an intelligent young man who needed a little guidance, and I wanted to help. Anthony became a big brother to Nicola and Traci throughout the years. He would often check out their boyfriends and give them advice. Or if they needed a ride, he was always around. Although Carl, Mitch, and Greg were older than Anthony and had a more secure family life, they became integral members of my family, brothers to my daughters, and forever friends.

BACK TO WORK

During my suspension from duty, the leadership of the SCCBFA shifted. I noticed they had become more conservative, politically savvy, and, at times, self-serving. Still, having known each of the new presidents personally—Angelo Chancellor, Clive Kennard, Booker Law, Bobby Dixon, and

Lacy Atkinson—I respected all of them. I also resumed a leadership role within the SCCBFA, though I never served as president again. Instead, I was elected vice president.

Despite the leadership change, they acknowledged that my direct, confrontational style remained crucial in advancing the interests of Black firefighters. For example, there was a promotional issue involving an SCCB-FA member that demanded our chapter's leadership intervention. A Santa Clara Fire Department fire captain had repeatedly passed promotional exams, ranking at the top of the list each time, yet was continually passed over for promotion. The SCCBFA president and other members met with the Santa Clara Fire Department, hoping to negotiate a resolution. With fire department brass on their side, they seemed well-positioned to succeed. But the department dismissed their concerns entirely. When the SCCBFA president asked me to attend the next meeting, I took a different approach. I confronted the department head-on, laying out the department's history and ongoing racism, and suggested that we bring in the federal government to intervene if necessary. My language was blunt, even vulgar, to drive the point home. I decided while on suspension that I would no longer waste time trying to communicate straightforward demands in the convoluted, bureaucratic language that white leadership often preferred.

My method worked. The captain was promoted to battalion chief and later hired as fire chief for the City of Santa Clara. However, after the meeting, several SCCBFA members expressed embarrassment over my aggressive style. They felt I had been too harsh and used language they couldn't support. Despite their discomfort, it wasn't the last time they asked for my help. They didn't approve of my tactics, but they couldn't deny the results.

Looking back on these events, and at the age of seventy-seven, I've become more knowledgeable, intuitive, and less naïve about the people I am involved with. I failed to take responsibility in key areas, instead choosing to aggressively confront the fire department, Black firefighters, and the union. Rather than heeding the warnings from Chief Clet, Dick Santos, and others, I became combative with nearly everyone—whether in the fire department, Local 873/230, the IABPFF, or the SCCBFA. The only person I showed consistent respect for was Lacy Atkinson. He possessed a level of insight I didn't have. While he understood my passion, he felt my approach—though effective—was too "ghetto."

My Brother, My Friend

By Lacy Atkinson

I RECEIVED A CALL during the last day of my recruit academy; the caller introduced himself as Dudley Bynoe and said he wanted to take me out to lunch. It was a sunny fall day when he rolled in front of the San Jose Fire Training Center with his black Cadillac Eldorado. On our way to lunch, we talked about my academic experience. He then began inquiring about the only other Black recruit who had been quietly fired on the last day of classwork. Our lunch was like a work meeting, he wanted to get as many facts as possible about the firefighter's performance at the academy from my perspective. His probing was laser focused. Afterward, he shared that he was off duty and fought for equal representation of Blacks in the fire service. He then said, "My friends call me Trusty."

During my probationary year, I watched Trusty fight these battles from my membership in the local union and the SCCBFA. He was usually the lone voice demanding equal and fair representation for minority fire-fighters. It was after those meetings that we would spend long hours in the evening discussing the issues facing the lack of women and minorities in the fire service and civil rights. His conviction to this cause was like none I'd ever experienced. It was at these meetings we learned we were kindred spir-its. We held Malcolm X up as our hero. Every year, on May 19, we would salute his birthday. I had wondered what the experience of walking with Malcolm and Martin would have been like; I found what that same convic-tion and commitment meant by walking with Trusty. He was willing to go anywhere at any time and speak with anybody about inequality and lack of minority representation. I feel fortunate to have witnessed his effectiveness; he got results.

When I completed my probationary year, he would ask me to accompany him when meeting with city and county executives to deal with issues of equity hiring. His method was direct and to the point; he spoke truth to power. I felt he was more like Kwame Ture (Stokley Carmichael); there was no compromise on the subject of equal and fair representation. He faced tremendous resistance, which became fuel for him to keep fighting, "Keep the fires burning for justice." Internationally, the fire service was changed by his relentless demand for minority representation. There was a minority affairs committee created by the International Association of Firefighters and local unions throughout the country that followed their lead. Locally, his calls for a change for the better are too many to note; four Black fire chiefs, women firefighters, representation of minorities in all ranks, and a safer workplace are a few of the changes that occurred because of Dudley's efforts.

After forty-three years of thousands of discussions and debates, he still had that same fire, concern, and commitment to equal hiring of minorities in the fire service. During our last conversation just hours before his passing, he happily shared the story of a young firefighter who had completed training, one of his mentees. That was Trusty.

Lacy Atkinson
Deputy fire chief, San Jose Fire Department
Past president, Santa Clara County Black Firefighters Association

Chapter 8

He Is a Thief

THIS CHAPTER DIVES DEEP into the complexities of leadership, betrayal, and perseverance during a pivotal era in Dudley's career. Upon returning to Station 16, Trusty faced hostility not only from white colleagues but also from Black firefighters, whose disloyalty fueled tensions. The promotion of Blain Owens as the first Black captain further emphasized the challenges of navigating internal politics and systemic racism. A major turning point involved the Tom Gray incident, where Trusty's relentless scrutiny of union finances exposed embezzlement, restoring accountability and reshaping his role within Local 873/230. The chapter also highlights Dudley's confrontational yet strategic partnership with City Manager Jerry Newfarmer, which ultimately led to the hiring of San Jose's first Black Fire Chief, Robert Osby. These events underscore the SCCBFA's influence in advancing equity, even amid fierce resistance. Additionally, the creation of the Minority Affairs Committee marked a significant step toward addressing the grievances of marginalized firefighters, despite union resistance. This chapter captures Trusty's unwavering determination to challenge injustice, rebuild trust, and empower those who sought change within the fire service.

When I returned to work at Station 16, I noticed a subtle shift in my crew's attitudes towards me. It quickly became evident that the San Jose Fire Department had conspired with the union (Local 873/230) to undermine the SCCBFA's membership. Local 873/230 members appeared less threatened by my challenges to their racist and white supremacist attitudes and statements. On several occasions, they would ignore me, a disrespect that infuriated me.

Some members of the SCCBFA also treated me with indifference. Several individuals I had considered allies seemed to harbor resentment against me, though they were careful to mask their feelings. While on duty, some Black firefighters would vilify me to their white counterparts. More than once, white firefighters contacted me directly to inform me of what had been said by these Black firefighters. When I confronted the Black men accused, they would acknowledge their disloyalty.

A major example of this power shift was the promotion of Blain Owens as the first Black captain. Owens, however, was not a supporter of the SCCBFA and did not represent our interests, which made it clear that I needed to reassert my leadership.

In 1984, while I was relaxing at home and watching television, I saw a news bulletin announcing that San Jose's City Manager, Jerry Newfarmer, was holding a press conference in forty-five minutes to address the city's loss of sixty million dollars due to bond irregularities. Without hesitation, I called Newfarmer's office and asked to speak with him directly. His secretary informed me that he was unavailable. I responded firmly, telling her to let him know that I would attend the press conference. While he was addressing the financial loss, I would publicly interrupt to demand answers about his "racist-ass fire department." Although I believed that consent decrees were often slow, ineffective, and did little to address real organizational change or foster respect for cultural differences, I threatened that Black firefighters would file one if significant improvements weren't made. Within ten to fifteen minutes, Newfarmer called back. He acknowledged that he knew who I was and what I had done for the fire service for the last thirteen years. He asked me not to attend the press conference but to come to his office the following day. I was pleased with his response. I was thirty-nine years old and still naïve enough to believe that a white man might want to make a difference. When I met with Newfarmer the next day, it was apparent that he did not want another city challenge. He immediately asked me to allow him time to improve conditions for the San Jose Fire Department's Black firefighters. He said I should file a consent decree if he had not made an appropriate change within six months. A consent decree would have consisted of hiring more Blacks, women, Latinos, and Asians based on the city's population and prior history of hiring. However, my initial belief was that consent decrees limited control of hiring to the white leadership, a plan I felt would lead to the hiring of Black men and women who had assimilated into white domination. I agreed to give him six months to make a substantial change that would help Black firefighters.

Within six months, Newfarmer fired Chief Clet, which upset me. Chief Clet was the first white chief who seemingly wanted to address racism in the fire department. While saddened by the sudden firing of Chief Clet, I knew that the San Jose fire chief position presented an opportunity for the SCCBFA to influence the selection of the next fire chief. The SCCBFA's connections with the IABPFF and the Southwest Region of the IABPFF had access to all current chief officers. This move would provide the SCCBFA an opportunity to find a Black chief officer in California, the nation's most diverse and wealthiest state.

Booker Law, a prominent member of the SCCBFA, sent Chief Robert Osby, the fire chief in Englewood, California, an application for the San Jose fire chief position. We met Osby in 1977 at the Marriott Hotel in Santa Clara, where the SCCBFA, under my presidency, hosted the International Association of Black Professional Fire Fighters Conference. Osby was the keynote speaker and addressed all the chapter presidents. Osby was an impressive speaker and a founding member of Brothers United, the San Diego chapter of the IABPFF. Booker and I became comrades because he recognized me as the driving force for change within the SCCBFA. As the regional director of the Southwest Region of the IABPFF, Booker was an arson investigator who inspired younger firefighters to pursue similar paths, and he had previously served as the president of the SCCBFA.

Booker reached out to Robert Osby three times, urging him to complete the application for the San Jose fire chief position. Working downtown, Booker leveraged his connections to stay informed about the application timeline. Ultimately, he contacted Osby just one day before the application deadline, insisting that he submit his application on time. In response, Robert Osby flew from San Diego to San Jose to deliver the application in person. Robert Osby became the San Jose fire chief in early 1985, Newfarmer kept his promise, and the San Jose Fire Department had its first Black fire chief. Many years later, Osby told me that Newfarmer told him to calm down Dudley Bynoe and help the department move forward with diversity and equity.

It was 1985, and Black people had become a force in every industry and career opportunity in the San Jose community. White people were eager to disrupt this fast-moving progress, which they assumed was the result of affirmative action policies. It was in the 1980s that President Reagan's administration reduced the budget of the Equal Opportunity Commission, attempted to disband the US Commission on Civil Rights, reduced the number of civil rights attorneys in the Justice Department, and urged the Supreme Court to end affirmative action.

After years of observing the leaders of Local 873/230 union, I grew concerned about how the organization's methods and procedures were managed, irrespective of their outcomes. Several executive board members were overly eager to maintain the status quo, routinely approving everything proposed by the leadership without questioning the effectiveness of the board itself. My next move was to become an executive board member to better observe the organization's management.

All members who wanted to run for a position on the executive board had to be nominated, campaign for the position, and be elected by union members. I believed I could not win a straight-up position on the executive board running against the white boys. I proposed that the executive board and its members form a Minority Affairs Committee to address the concerns of people of color and women. First, I had to get Local 873/230 to approve the committee. Even though many Local 873/230 members disliked my presence, some recognized the issues with diversity and equity in the fire department and thought my idea might benefit the membership. For several months, I visited every San Jose fire station on all three shifts, with a few white union members helping me promote my idea to other union members and secure their votes. When the union met, firefighters voted to add an unpaid Minority Affairs Committee (MAC) to their board.

However, the union's executive board resisted the MAC because it entailed changing the International Association of Fire Fighters (IAFF) bylaws. The president of Local 873/230, Ken Heredia, suggested I write a resolution, take it to the entire body of the IAFF, and request them to make the necessary bylaw change. I worked with a knowledgeable white firefighter to write a formal resolution. I presented the resolution before the entire body of the IAFF (all white men) in Kansas City, Missouri. The IAFF rejected the resolution that would have required every fire department's local union throughout the United States to establish an MAC as part of their executive board. However, Ken Heredia agreed to allow the executive board to vote on establishing the committee. San Jose union members voted affirmatively to create a MAC representing all minorities, which included

African Americans, Latinos, Asians, and women. Because the IAFF failed to pass the resolution, the MAC chairs could advise the executive board but were nonpaid executive board members.

After establishing the MAC, Ken Heredia, the current union president, canvassed for volunteers to represent each minority group. I volunteered for the job, and one other Black firefighter also stepped forward to serve and represent Black firefighters. Although I had established the committee, union leaders attempted to undermine my efforts by replacing me with another Black firefighter. Their first choice was someone who seemed more interested in advancing his career than in protecting the rights and addressing the grievances of Black firefighters; in other words, the union was looking for a Clarence Thomas–type leader. I spoke privately with the union's preferred candidate and convinced him to withdraw his application for the MAC representative position. Consequently, I became the first MAC member to represent Black firefighters in the San Jose Fire Department.

During my first year as a MAC chair my purpose was to attend all executive board meetings and observe everything the leadership did. I knew that Heredia was my number one antagonist. So, I watched the financials, the donations to charities, politician endorsements, contract negotiations, and the members' attitudes towards communities of color and women. I suspected that some irregular methods and dealings were going on. They had a tremendous amount of money. Local 873/230 rarely gave funds to minority organizations or supported their agendas, such as affirmative action policies, the NAACP, Mexican organizations, women's organizations, or other non-white and non-male organizations. I made it my duty to attend their political fundraisers and union-hosted events at prestigious historical sites and prominent politicians' homes. I participated in an event at the mayor's house; it was immediately evident that I was not welcomed. The event was staged in the backyard, where the temperature was close to one hundred degrees; I remember having the top two buttons of my shirt open. One of the union officers approached me and said, "You are exposing yourself." Of course, I ignored him and did not button my shirt. These events were interesting. They revealed the political power of Local 873/230. I discovered that the union had funded and influenced several local and state elections.

After working on the executive board for the MAC and having a good rapport with the San Jose Fire Department, several white members suggested they would nominate, campaign, and vote for me to be a full-time paid executive board member. The lowest-paid executive board position was that of the trustee. I led the MAC for several years; then, I selected a replacement, Lacy Atkinson, who I knew would express and protect Black firefighters' concerns.

Throughout the years, Black firefighters anonymously complained about racist statements on bulletin boards and the severe unequal treatment imposed on them in their stations. Some of the new firefighters feared associating their names with formal complaints and instead would ask me to investigate the situations and, if appropriate, file a formal complaint. When I was informed that a Black firefighter would be disciplined, I explored the situation and talked to their supervisor and the firefighter. However, I was not official. Usually, after meeting with all parties, I convinced the supervisor of less punitive options to avoid the dissolution of the firefighters' careers. Linda was impressed by my progress; she suggested that since I knew several San Jose college and university professors, I should take a class or two to broaden my vocabulary and writing skills. I took her advice and enrolled in Charles Murray's Ethnic Studies class, where I was encouraged to speak about my life experiences. Linda and I lectured at the Black Student Union (BSU) events on relationships, education, and San Jose's Black community.

I ran for my first paid position with Local 873/230 as a trustee on the executive board of the union in 1990 and won. During my first year as trustee, I was responsible for assessing and ensuring all union bills were paid. While reviewing the union's accounts, I discovered discrepancies that I couldn't fully understand due to my limited knowledge of accounting methodology. I approached the treasurer, Tom Gray, with questions about the finances of Local 873/230 and requested an audit of the books. Initially, Tom resisted, claiming it was unnecessary. I then proposed hiring an independent auditor to help us understand the accounting process and validate the accuracy of our balance sheets. The union president deemed it an unnecessary expense and declined my request. Anyone who knows me knows that the union's decision to deny my bid led to a heated verbal confrontation.

At monthly membership meetings, I expressed concern about how union money was used, causing some members to question union leaders. After they rejected my request for an audit, I began criticizing the treasurer every chance I got. I called him out with accusations, "You are a thief, lying crook, and dirty motherfucker." I must have challenged him in this fashion thirty times before he broke down crying. He admitted to his crimes of misappropriation of funds.[1] It became apparent that the former trustees were inept in their duties or did not care enough to challenge the leadership.

After the treasurer resigned, Ken Heredia, the Local 873/230 president, handed over all the treasurer's books to me as a form of punishment. In response, I requested that the executive board hire an independent auditor to examine the records. To assist with this task, I approached two firefighters, Sam Francisco and Richard Santos, to help me identify the best auditors in town. Sam Francisco, a real estate tycoon and astute businessman, diligently sought out a qualified auditor. I developed a relationship with Francisco early in my career when I became a permanent firefighter, and he stood up for me at the beginning of my career. Santos was a firm union member who worked with me on several projects. With Santos and Francisco's assistance, we were able to find an independent auditor who would evaluate the books, correct any discrepancies, and establish a process to prevent future misconduct.

Getting the treasurer's books corrected reestablished my political power and allowed me to be voted in as one of the three shift representatives. Shift representatives were responsible for all firefighters on their shift and were required to address all disciplinary actions. As an executive board member, I was paid for my time and could propose suggestions to the executive board on ways to improve employee relationships with the City of San Jose.

To become a shift representative, I had to visit every station, every shift, fire administration, fire prevention bureau, and the training center to convince all union members that I would represent them impartially. Several firefighters acknowledged my negotiation wisdom and felt as a shift representative, I would be an asset to all firefighters. Most firefighters with grievances about working conditions received favorable resolutions under my guidance

1. The incident was then reported on in the *Mercury News*. See Gray, "Union Funds Taken."

My Brother, My Friend

By Russell Steppe

It was in 1983 when I attended my first Black firefighters' conference. The IABPFF's Southwest Region members had gathered in Phoenix, Arizona, to support the local Black firefighters as they formed what would become the Heat Wave Black Firefighters Association.

As a new firefighter with just a year of experience, I walked into the hotel conference room. I was struck by the sight of approximately sixty tall Black men, dressed in suits and exuding professionalism and strength. Each group represented a Black firefighter association from major city fire departments in California, Nevada, and Arizona. Being in that conference filled me with pride, seeing my brothers who understood my struggles as a Black firefighter and shared my passion for the job.

Among the attendees, one man stood out. He had a commanding presence and a strong voice. I soon learned his name was Dudley "Trusty" Bynoe. When you meet someone new, you often look for common ground. With Trusty, I noticed we both wore the same kind of dress shoes: "Biscuits" Stacy Adams, popular among older Black men at the time. Little did I know that I had just met my lifelong brother in the fire service.

That day, Trusty became my Black firefighter big brother. As our friendship grew, we traveled to many cities across America, met up when we got there, and wherever we went, he taught me to live up to the IABPFF's motto to "Keep the fires burning for justice." Trusty was passionate about improving conditions for men and women in fire departments. While his approach was confrontational, his goal was always progress and equality, reminiscent of Malcolm X's philosophy of achieving change by any means necessary.

Trusty hailed from the San Jose Fire Department. Over time, he became as close to me, if not closer, than my biological brothers. Proverbs 18:24 says, "A man who has friends must himself be friendly, but there is a friend who sticks closer than a brother." Over the next thirty-nine years, I got to know Trusty and his family—Linda, Nicky, and Traci—the Bynoes.

Trusty was extremely intelligent, strong, confident, and supportive of his fellow Black firefighters. If someone faced issues with the authorities in their city, Trusty would always make himself available to assist in any way he could. As Black firefighters, we all encountered systemic racism, and through the legal system, we continued to fight for racial and gender equality and justice.

We met at Southwest Regional conferences twice yearly in various cities. Putting alpha-type, aggressive Black men in a room often led to serious disagreements. Trusty, usually the loudest and most passionate person in the room, would stir things up and then use the tension in the room to unite us, bring us together so we could focus our efforts and be united against common challenges. His leadership and strategic thinking were invaluable to our Black firefighter organizations.

Trusty was dedicated to the IABPFF cause, respected in San Jose, throughout the Southwest Region, and nationwide. He was recognized within the IAFF, honored in his community, and trusted by many. Most importantly, Trusty was a devoted family man and a proud "girl dad."

Trusty's passion for improving opportunities for Blacks and people of color in the fire service extended to helping women of color. I remember his relationship with Teresa Reed when she joined the San Jose Fire Department. He made it clear that we should respect her, and we did, as we were all fighting to get sisters of all colors into our fire departments.

Trusty understood that to win the battles Black firefighters faced, we needed to engage from within the firefighter organizations, especially the unions that often opposed us. Black firefighters across the country were paying dues to unions that did not represent them fairly. Trusty decided to work from within, starting with his local union and then moving on to the national IAFF scene.

On several occasions, I found myself outside IAFF meetings or conventions, picketing with my IABPFF brothers against the IAFF union's disparate treatment of its Black, people of color, and women members. As we pushed for justice and equality from the outside, Trusty pushed for justice and equality from the inside, leading to real changes within the IAFF.

I recall an incident at an IAFF Human Relations conference that was held in Indianapolis, Indiana. It was the first time I attended an IAFF conference on the inside as a registrant. After a heated morning session meeting, Trusty and I went outside during the break to get some fresh air and to calm down.

As we came in from outside, we entered the elevator and encountered two of the Boston firefighters who had been very vocal in the meeting. While stepping in, one of the Boston guys gave Trusty a sideways look and it was immediately on. Trusty stepped to that guy and I stepped to the other Boston guy.

As the elevator doors closed Trusty was all up in that guy's face saying, "Yeah, you think you're a bad motherfucker. Now what's your bitch ass gotta say? And please say how you feel, so I can fuck you up." The more Trusty spoke, the redder the guy's face became. And the louder Trusty got, the spray of his breath specked the guy's face.

Just before the elevator got to their floor, the Boston guys became very shaky, and they were very apologetic as they exited the elevator. Of course, we laughed as the doors closed and we continued our elevator ride. When we exited the elevator, Trusty turned to me and said, "We may lose some of these battles, but I guarantee we will win the war." For the rest of that conference, those Boston guys were very respectful, and we were respectful too. We even shook hands at the end of the conference.

Being a warrior is taxing, and in this life, we all face betrayals. As Trusty's career with the San Jose Fire Department ended, new opportunities arose for him to be there for his family and community. He remained in contact with those of us still working.

In retirement, Trusty and I stayed close, talking almost daily, laughing, joking, and being silly, just like we did in fire stations across the country. When I faced breast cancer, Trusty looked out for me, called and cared for me, and I am forever grateful that God blessed me with my brother Trusty. I miss you, bro.

Russell Steppe
Captain/fire investigator
Brother's United, San Diego Black Firefighters Inc.
San Diego Fire-Rescue Department

Chapter 9

Generational Reciprocity

THIS CHAPTER DELVES INTO the transformative work of the SCCBFA during the 1980s and early 1990s, a period marked by significant growth, political engagement, and community impact. Leaders like Booker Law, Bobby Dixon, and Lacy Atkinson steered the organization toward fostering Black representation in fire service leadership while championing city politics and community programs. Their efforts not only bolstered the recruitment of Black firefighters but also supported the rise of influential Black leaders in local and state governance.

Amid the SCCBFA's public successes, internal tensions arose regarding its future direction—balancing activism with professional development. As systemic racism persisted, the organization faced challenges in sustaining unity and purpose. Dudley's unyielding advocacy and mentorship were central to navigating these struggles, ensuring the SCCBFA remained a force for social justice. This chapter reflects on the organization's achievements, challenges, and the enduring fight for equity within the fire service, while raising critical questions about generational reciprocity, solidarity, and the price of progress.

Throughout the next ten-plus years, leaders of the SCCBFA supported political and social changes within the fire service and the community. Booker Law served as the regional director of the Southwest Region of the IABPFF. Bobby Dixon encouraged firefighters to engage in city politics and take on leadership roles within their fire departments. He became a member of the Board of Trustees for Mission College, representing the area of fire science, and was always willing to mentor any member aspiring to advance within the fire service.

Lacy Atkinson focused on grooming young Black firefighters to lead community youth programs and actively campaigned for Black city and state candidates. Notable figures he supported include Iola Williams, the first Black city councilwoman; Cathy Cole, the second Black city councilwoman; LaDoris Cordell, the first Black woman judge in Santa Clara County; and Regina Williams, the first Black woman to be San Jose city manager, and others throughout the state.

The SCCBFA continued its recruitment efforts, offering training classes and hosting career days for elementary through high school students. They also participated in community events like the NAACP, Juneteenth festivals, and other local organizations. At these events, the SCCBFA staffed information booths to promote firefighter recruitment and fire safety. They offered career development workshops, fire safety education, and adult health classes.

During the 1980s, the SCCBFA became more politically active, with several members elected to or invited to various boards and organizations. This was a time of tremendous growth for the organization—events were consistently sold out, annual dances were held at prestigious hotels, and yearly retreats took place in Carmel Valley, California. Sponsored by the IABPFF in 1991, the SCCBFA brought the largest group of Black firefighters to the Executive Development Institute (EDI) inauguration at Florida A&M University in Tallahassee, Florida.

My support for every SCCBFA president was unwavering; my commitment had been the driving force behind the organization. It was my militant approach that had disrupted the system and transformed the fire service. My activism continued to challenge city leadership, local unions—particularly San Jose's—and their hiring and promotional practices. I demanded fair and consistent treatment for Black firefighters. Additionally, I focused on creating recruitment pathways that significantly increased the number of Black firefighters in our county. These efforts inspired other firefighter organizations and departments to actively include and hire men and women of color. The departments most impacted by the SCCBFA's recruitment program included Palo Alto, Milpitas, Santa Clara, Sunnyvale, Mountain View, and many others throughout the Southwest. Our recruitment efforts also had a ripple effect, influencing other ethnic groups, such as Mexicans (Los Bomberos), Asian Americans in the fire service, and women (NorCal Women in the Fire Service), showcasing the widespread success and impact of the SCCBFA.

While the SCCBFA's public profile grew, we faced an internal struggle: Should we remain a militant activist organization fighting for social justice or shift towards a focus on professional development and advancement within the fire service? As more Black firefighters were promoted to captain, I noticed a shift from group solidarity to individualism. Some members used the SCCBFA as a stepping stone for career advancement, showing up for photo opportunities but failing to attend meetings, participate in recruiting, or support Black communities.

Meanwhile, younger Black firefighters often only approached me when they were in trouble, while showing deference to Black captains. On the other hand, white leaders in the fire service, feeling threatened by Black success, began to show resentment and sought ways to undermine policies that had fostered Black firefighter advancement. I firmly believed this was not the time to become complacent or "bougie"; we needed to stay true to our activist roots.

I was challenged to understand the younger brothers and sisters and what they stood for. Were our youth aspiring to accept a caste system, an attitude that assumed the same hatred and discrimination the first Black firefighters had endured? Were white fire chiefs hiring Black men and women who had acculturated or accepted systems of discrimination? Or were the young Black people hired unaware of their history and the value of fighting against anti-Black racism? It appeared the younger Black firefighters lacked an understanding of generational reciprocity. Often, young Black firefighters apologized for their part in denigrating me while conferring with their white firefighter friends; when I approached them for their duplicity, they were usually embarrassed and apologetic. I tried to explain that they were assimilating and seeing themselves through a lens of whiteness and that their self-esteem would eventually be deflated. I often lectured them about how anti-Black, racist attitudes only perpetuate an acceptance of a caste system as old as time, irrespective of their economic or educational status. What sustained me to continue fighting for Black firefighters' rights throughout those years was the respect, support, and awards received from the SCCBFA and many of San Jose's Black community leaders. However, several things made me question some of the SCCBFA leaders' loyalty to the organization.

I remained busy working to resolve heated conflicts among firefighters. I remained a staunch advocate for Black firefighters' respectful and equitable treatment. However, many white firefighters were opponents of affirmative action: the law, they argued, was the only reason Black people were hired, ultimately causing an abundance of reverse discrimination laws throughout the country by 1996. The increase in hiring Black firefighters caused more occurrences of racist events in fire stations, training centers, the fire administration, and the union hall. They frequently spoke negatively to Black firefighters, questioning their abilities to perform, noting openly that Black firefighters only got the jobs because of affirmative action. The fire service, much like many militaristic organizations, was riddled with physical and verbal altercations. When confrontations involved Black and white firefighters, the blame was often directed at the Black firefighters. Even when white firefighters made microaggressive comments toward their Black colleagues, Black firefighters were expected to walk away and not engage. Younger firefighters were more likely to resort to physical confrontations. Still, these altercations were usually defused by the crew, often at the expense of the Black firefighters, who were unjustly condemned.

I was discouraged because Black youth were not aware of our African principles: generational reciprocity, spirituality, and activism. Generational reciprocity relates to our ability to accept our elders' knowledge and life experiences. Our elders' tasks are to pass on our history and culture and to groom our youth for leadership. The second principle is spirituality (not necessarily religious), meaning those inherent talents that are indigenous to our personhood and our interdependence, interconnection, and integration with each other and the earth. And last but not least, the principle of activism: our ancestors fought against injustice for centuries throughout Africa and the world. I believe that many of our youth were not raised to understand that these principles reflect our relevance to the era.

Historically, when Black people lose their guiding principles, power struggles, jealousy, and disrespect are the undercurrents that kill organizations and weaken our resolve. For example, under the leadership of the president of the IABPFF, Clarence Williams was the victim of a coup that drastically and, I believe, unfathomably damaged the IABPFF. Misinformation floated throughout the IABPFF, suggesting missing funds, prompting a smear campaign to defeat Clarence Williams. Some of the leaders of the coup were jealous of Williams's popularity. He was single, wealthy, and had been acknowledged by *Ebony* magazine as one of the most eligible bachelors in the country. Williams was connected politically with Washington,

DC, and brought legitimacy to the IABPFF at the highest levels. He was the first IABPFF president to protest the IAFF (the white organization).

I worried that my generation of firefighters, those intricately involved with the struggles of getting Black men and women hired, were also the lead conspirators in the demise of the IABPFF. The main perpetrators had reached chief officers' positions and had status within the IABPFF. One of the most egregious instances of disregard for the IABPFF was when a group of Black firefighters altered the EDI program's purpose, ultimately turning it into a for-profit business. This change in policy and programming weakened the IABPFF; the EDI was the conduit that brought all the regions together. I believe that the original purpose of the EDI was to grant Black firefighters an opportunity to learn from other Black firefighters who mastered specific leadership skills that helped or affected Black firefighters, and to support the financial needs of the IABPFF. Instead, EDI became an education facility for all firefighters, including white firefighters, at the cost of paid instructors.

I also admired Bill Brown, a chief officer of the Federal Fire Service in San Diego, California. He was the first and only person to create and sell Black firefighters' paraphernalia, lapel pins and tie clips, cuff links, and other jewelry at all IABPFF conferences. I think Brown was heartbroken by the radical change in the IABPFF, the dissolution of the original purpose of the EDI, and the elimination of his products dedicated to promoting the unity of Black firefighters. His creations were radical in the fire service. It was the only paraphernalia that represented Black firefighters in the United States. The loss of Bill Brown was another example of the slow demise of the IABPFF. I liked most of the people involved in the coup, but their blind allegiance to one man, Carl Holmes, led to an extreme decrease in regional participation and support of the IABPFF. After the coup succeeded, EDI was the only viable program available for the IABPFF.

NO PROMOTION FOR DUDLEY BYNOE

After working many years as a firefighter, I became proficient in fighting fires. Eighty-five percent of the calls received in San Jose were EMS calls. I was permanently assigned to the Light Unit, so I worked with several different fire engineers, and in later years, I was privileged to work with Roland Hooks, a Black engineer. During that time, EMS calls were handled by the truck company, specifically the secondary unit, which was called the Light Unit.

We handled vehicle accidents, heart attacks, childbirth, gunshot wounds, and drug overdoses. I often worked in the acting captain position when the captain was unavailable. Several captains and Linda encouraged me to take the captain's exam. Linda had her master's degree and offered to study with me, but I declined; it was an ego thing. I was on two promotional lists for the captain position, both times under the leadership of two Black fire chiefs.

The testing process included a written test and an oral interview. Two Black training captains were involved in creating the tests. The deputy chief of training was ultimately responsible for the final examinations. Although I passed the tests twice, I never achieved high enough scores. I was asked by the deputy chief officer of training, "Didn't you get a copy of the test?" It was well-known throughout the San Jose Fire Department that a select group of white firefighters received a copy when the tests were written. I respected both training officers, but their lack of trust and care for me hurt.

White battalion chiefs who worked throughout Santa Clara County often served as raters for the promotional oral board interview process. On numerous occasions, I challenged several of these white chief officers who sat on my oral boards. For instance, two of the white chief officers on one of my oral boards were from a department where two SCCBFA leaders and I had previously attended a meeting. At that meeting, they had denied the promotion of a Black fire captain to battalion chief despite him ranking number one on all tests. I threatened to involve the federal government to establish a consent decree and used strong, confrontational rhetoric to challenge the city manager, fire administration officers, and other city leaders. As a result, the wronged captain was promoted to battalion chief.

While I passed the oral boards twice, my scores kept me out of hiring reach. Although I had seniority, which added extra points to my score, I still needed to be rated higher. Some white captains were shocked by my scores. They felt I should have been promoted. When new captains came to my station, they relied on me to make critical decisions during emergency calls. Battalion chiefs would confer with me about overhaul operations, confirming the fire was out. There was nothing more embarrassing than having a rekindle (a fire reigniting after it was determined to be extinguished).

MY RELATIONSHIP WITH CHIEF OSBY

Many Black firefighters failed to recognize that the lack of respect for Chief Osby's leadership stemmed from anti-Black racism. Anti-Black racism is the perpetuation of American classism; it predetermines the socioeconomic status of Blacks in this country and is held in place by anti-Black policies, institutions, and ideologies. While Black firefighters admired Osby's professional demeanor, intellectual discourse, and confident attitude, they feared showing allegiance to him in front of their white colleagues. Although Chief Osby maintained an open-door policy, few Black firefighters took the initiative to meet with him. He actively attended many SCCBFA functions, dances, retreats, and community events to demonstrate his support for Black firefighters.

When newly hired white firefighters disparaged Chief Osby, making derogatory remarks such as hiring a Black chief was purely an affirmative action decision, I would threaten to inform Chief Osby. If I overhead negative statements from veteran firefighters, I lectured them harshly about their racism. I continued to keep Chief Osby abreast of attitudes and behaviors and the overall climate of the white firefighters. Chief Osby brilliantly started a regular Chief's Chat program with this information. Chief's Chat was a closed-circuit television program available for those firefighters on and off duty. Any firefighter could call in with questions or concerns about work-related problems. Chief Osby convened the program in the training center so firefighters could participate face-to-face with the chief. The Chief Chat theme song was "I Heard It Through the Grape Vine" by Gladys Knight and The Pips. When Chief Osby addressed Latinos, he spoke in Spanish, highlighting his multilingual abilities.

Chief Osby recognized that the San Jose Fire Department was derelict in hiring women firefighters. Karen Kirsch was the first woman hired in San Jose under Chief Clet. Five years later, Chief Osby hired six women in January 1986 and another four women in October 1986. Teresa Deloach Reed was the first African American woman firefighter hired for the City of San Jose Fire Department. Karen Kirsch (Allen) later retired as a battalion chief. Teresa Reed had completed the SCCBFA classes; Reed took the civil service exam, passed it with a high score, and was placed on the City of San Jose Firefighters' hiring list. Chief Osby hired Reed in 1986. Teresa was the first woman in the history of the San Jose Fire Department to be promoted to engineer, captain, battalion chief, deputy chief, and assistant fire chief. She later became the first woman to hold the position of fire chief in Oakland, California. My experience with Reed was that of a mentor and protector. She often disagreed with me but, when necessary, had my back, and I had hers.

Reed and I fought a fully involved kitchen fire together, a challenging fire because of its proximity to other homes and the amount of heat and debris she was exposed to. This fire helped Reed determine her future in the fire service. After we put the fire out and removed our helmets and self-contained breathing apparatus face pieces, Reed shook her hair and said, "Trust, I am not doing this anymore." I perceived her statement to mean she was not getting dirty and wet fighting fires; she wanted to be a leader. The next time I saw Reed, she was a fire engineer. Reed had learned the basis for getting promoted. She successfully utilized the training resources provided by the SCCBFA and the IABPFF. She had worked within the white patriarchal system and flourished. Chief Osby exuded a brilliance that changed the disposition of many of his officers, one that trickled down to first-line supervisors, the captains. I observed Chief Osby end one of his deputy chiefs' careers. The deputy chief disrespected Osby by refusing to adhere to a demand, a privilege many white firefighters had shown Black captains in the past. Chief Osby, aware of the deputy's perspective, told the deputy chief that he was releasing him from his duties and expected him to do nothing daily but show up to work and stay in his office. Ultimately, Chief Osby assumed the deputy chief's duties. The consequences of Chief Osby's actions were that the deputy chief retired, and his command staff understood that there would be no disrespect, that all orders from Chief Robert Osby would be carried out swiftly and efficiently, and that no mistakes would occur or be tolerated. While I was aware of Chief Osby's decision to punish the deputy chief, I disagreed vehemently with his choice of who was the most disrespectful person on his staff. This disagreement erupted in harsh words between Chief Osby and me, resulting in my being kicked out of his office.

Chief Osby had all the attributes that endeared him to white firefighters, i.e., being college educated, a good speaker, handsome, innovative, politically conservative, and understanding how to use power. Unfortunately, he never had a Black firefighter's organization with the esteem, political, and community power to protect and challenge him. Three SCCBFA members had Chief Osby's ear: Russell Hayden, a San Jose Fire Department friend; Bobby Dixon from Milpitas Fire Department, a political companion; and me, a social justice advocate who challenged him most often.

I viewed Chief Osby as a pivotal figure in my firefighting career. Under his leadership, my skills flourished, I observed how Osby controlled white men using the power of his badge to dismantle their privilege. My position on the Union Local 873/230 Executive Board advanced rapidly, and my creativity thrived. My close relationship with Chief Osby, along with the support of other firefighters, enabled me to play a crucial role in establishing a comprehensive support system for firefighters, addressing their mental health and substance abuse issues. John Laurent, Dennis Madigan, Dick Toledo, and I were instrumental in creating a robust support network. They understood my reluctance to work on Christmas holidays due to a traumatic experience in 1974 when I had discovered five children dead in a house fire. Together, we developed the Employee Assistance Program (EAP), which offered critical stress debriefing, post-traumatic stress counseling, and psychological support.

Recognizing that several firefighters struggled with drug and alcohol addiction, we knew we needed to help them. Chief Osby appointed me, as chair of the EAP, to travel to Chicago and San Francisco to study the effects of substance abuse. During the Chicago meetings at a drug counseling center, we discussed key issues with substance abuse counselors, focusing on success rates and relapse triggers. They shared insights on potential triggers for substance use after leaving treatment centers and suggested processes and medications that departments should have available to support healthy recovery.

The most valuable information I gathered included the names and addresses of top care facilities in California, which had high success rates and follow-up systems to help combat addiction. My committee compiled a report that assisted the San Jose Fire Department and Chief Osby in launching a drug assistance program for San Jose firefighters. With the assistance of Dick Toledo, Dennis Madigan, and John Laurent, who were crucial board members, we worked to build programs that helped firefighters navigate social and family challenges. This collaboration between Chief Osby and the City of San Jose, the Union Local 873/230, and the EAP strengthened relationships and fostered tremendous respect for our department.

In 1992, Chief Osby left the San Jose Fire Department to become the fire chief of the City of San Diego, where he had started his career. One of the significant reasons Chief Osby left San Jose was because he had several hostile encounters with the new Assistant City Manager, Regina Williams. Losing Chief Osby meant that Black firefighters' protections were diminished. I felt that the attacks on the IABPFF and the loss of Chief Osby were the end of my career. The SCCBFA honored Chief Osby with an honorary membership and the SCCBFA jacket.

Chapter 10

Girl Dad

"GIRL DAD" EXPLORES THE complexities of fatherhood, identity, and the profound responsibility Dudley felt in shaping his daughters' lives. From a young age, both of his daughters saw their dad as a hero, a label that Dudley embraced and questioned as he navigated his role as a father. The chapter opens with a dramatic moment in Seaside, where Dudley unexpectedly rescues two children from a burning apartment, a heroic act that leaves him both proud and conflicted. While the San Jose Fire Department questioned his decision, Dudley was humbled by the local recognition and proud of the way his daughters viewed him.

This chapter also delves into Dudley's personal growth as a father, particularly through his evolving relationship with Traci and Nicola. As his daughters matured, each of them faced challenges that tested the family dynamics and Dudley's ability to be the father they needed. Whether it was navigating Traci's entrepreneurial spirit and love interest or supporting Nicola through her educational struggles, Dudley constantly challenged what it meant to be a "girl dad." The chapter also reflects on the impact of his leadership in the fire service, particularly at Station 16, where Dudley worked to build a community that mirrored the values he hoped to instill in his daughters. As Dudley looks back, he realizes that while he worked hard to protect and provide for his daughters, he missed many opportunities to be the father they needed in other ways—something Dudley came to understand more deeply as he explored the intersections of race and gender.

From a young age, my daughters have always viewed me as a hero. One weekend, while visiting my mother-in-law in Monterey, I fell ill and was recovering in an upstairs bedroom. I called my station to inform the captain that I was not well. As I rested in bed, I heard my daughters burst into my mother-in-law's apartment, screaming that their friends in the apartment across from us were trapped in a fire. Still groggy, I told them to have their grandmother call the fire department. Without a second thought, I jumped out of bed, still in my pajamas, and ran outside. I could hear the children screaming—trapped in one of the upstairs bedrooms. The downstairs portion of the apartment was filled with smoke; covering my nose and mouth with a towel, I followed the sound of the children's cries. When I reached the bedroom, I found two children huddled together in a corner under a blanket. I grabbed them, wrapped the blanket tightly around them, and carried them downstairs and out the front door. As we got outside, I could hear the fire truck approaching Broadway. The Seaside Fire Department arrived just in time to put the fire out; they found that the fire started in the kitchen. The firefighters were impressed by what I had done. I later received a letter from Seaside's fire chief acknowledging my actions, and the *Monterey Herald* published a positive article about the incident. Though I initially worried about entering the apartment without safety gear, I was grateful that I could act quickly. Most of all, I was proud that my daughters (little girls at the time) saw me as the hero. The San Jose Fire Department had a different take on my hero's actions. They felt that if I was well enough to save the two Black children in Seaside, I should have been at work saving San Jose residents.

While both of my daughters were daddy's girls, Traci shared more of my youthful tendencies than Nicola. Traci was the type to do whatever she wanted, accepting the consequences when caught. On the other hand, Nicola tried to avoid serious trouble but often found herself involved with the wrong men—a problem I could resolve quickly.

Linda successfully managed a demanding job at Pacific Bell while pursuing her master's degree in education at the University of San Francisco. Our intense focus on providing our daughters with everything we deemed essential caused us to overlook some significant dangers and influences that impacted them. Linda actively encouraged me to take classes at one of the community colleges but I encountered challenges in finding the discipline to take on more than one class at a time. Nevertheless, I was invited by professors at San Jose City College and Evergreen Community

College to deliver lectures on the history of Black men in the fire service throughout the United States.

Nicola graduated from James Lick High School, where she lettered in track and basketball and earned an associate of arts degree from Mission College. Traci graduated from Overfelt High School, becoming the first-string center on the girls' basketball team. She briefly attended San Jose City College, where she earned several business certificates, including one in tax preparation. Over the years, Traci became an entrepreneur, owning a hair salon, a trucking company, and a tax preparation service in San Jose. We were proud when she married her baby's father and embraced her entrepreneurial spirit.

When the girls played high school sports, I made it a point to attend all of Traci's basketball games because she played the position of first-string center. I was Overfelt's biggest fan, though my booming voice often annoyed the coaches, especially when it clashed with their instructions. I also attended as many of Nicola's basketball games as possible, sometimes driving between the two schools on the same evening. Nicola was second-string guard but seldom had an opportunity to play; she also ran track, and I never missed those events, needing to encourage her to the finish line.

Linda relied on me to serve as a protector and to help guide our daughters in their life choices. I took this responsibility to heart, particularly recognizing her leniency and her concerns about the girls being tempted to follow in the footsteps of our siblings. Both Linda and I had siblings who faced severe drug problems, and we were determined to shield our daughters from a similar fate. Drawing from my upbringing, I adopted the role of disciplinarian, believing it would help keep them safe. We thought that maintaining a firm hand would prevent them from straying down the wrong path. Thankfully, our daughters were never drawn to drugs, having witnessed the devastation they caused our family. However, we encountered other challenges—teen pregnancy, truancy, relationships with gangster boyfriends, car accidents, and periods when they would go missing for days.

During those challenging years, Linda worked as a manager at Pacific Bell and commuted to the Bay Area. She wanted to provide our daughters with everything they needed; both girls attended private schools and had their own spaces and cars. We never wanted them to rely on someone else for transportation. I knew I had to buckle down and focus on supporting them while improving their futures. There were times when I wasn't sure our marriage would survive. I felt like I had failed as the girls' dad.

However, despite our struggles, Linda and the girls knew that I would risk my life to protect them and do whatever it took to keep them safe—even if it meant going to extremes to defend them from harm.

Meanwhile, Linda completed her doctor of education degree and challenged herself to co-teach a class at the University of San Francisco while working at Pacific Bell. She was incredibly busy but wanted desperately to change careers. While Linda was a loving mother, she was not always aware of the girls' needs. When Traci got pregnant and gave birth to a daughter I tried my best to be a good grandfather, a better father, and a supportive husband.

STATION 16: A BLACK FIRE STATION

During Chief Osby's tenure, I took the initiative to establish a predominantly Black fire station by recruiting Black firefighters to Station 16. Chief Osby was concerned that creating what might be seen as a segregated station would be a step backward, considering the fire service's history of racial segregation, where Black firefighters were restricted to specific stations. He often referenced the mistreatment of Black firefighters in cities like Los Angeles, San Diego, and Oakland in the early twentieth century, believing that a segregated station in the 1990s would hinder progress toward equality. However, I saw it differently. Black firefighters had earned the seniority and the right to choose where they wanted to work. If they preferred to be at a station with others who shared their cultural background, they now had the same opportunity as their white counterparts. In my view, this wasn't regression—it was progress, as we exercised our right to choose where and with whom we worked.

Station 16's C shift included me, Captain Don Bell, Dick Kirkham, Doug Potter, Henry Mendoza, Ron Pomerantz, and Bobby Wells. We worked well together, but new positions would open as people transferred or got promoted. Others could use their seniority to bid for the spot when that happened. The first person I reached out to about an opening was Roland Hooks. When he spoke to Captain Bell about the opportunity, Bell told him to check with me first—a moment we still laugh about today. I had the opportunity to work with many fire captains: Jerry Floyd, Blain Owens, Mel Meeks, and Bobby Wells on the Engine Company, and George Long, Don Bell, and Philip Broussard on the Truck Company. I'm not sure why Jerry Floyd chose my station during my shift, but he was the first white captain who spoke to me with respect and made an effort to understand my anger and fight against racism.

As more positions became available, I continued to seek out Black firefighters to join us. Some were hesitant, concerned about how white colleagues might perceive them. Others were comfortable where they were, not wanting to disrupt the friendships they had built. Some, however, were curious about the station's possibilities. One Black captain bid for a spot, hoping to make a name for himself by educating and "whipping the Black firefighters into shape." Meanwhile, some of my friends and colleagues trusted my leadership and bid on the station because of that trust.

The highlight of my career came when Black firefighters dominated Station 16. The culture transformed—our food, music, and conversations reflected Black culture. For the first time, I didn't feel the need to defend Blackness or explain our experiences. I never missed a day of work, never got sick, and was never late. It was an exciting, fulfilling time as we grew together like a family. Many of us worked out together, lifted weights, played basketball, and mentored younger Black firefighters. Station 16 also became a gathering place for the local community. Young Black and Latino kids often visited, sharing meals with us, playing pool, and discussing their lives. Most importantly, they felt welcomed. Teachers and parents even sought us out to speak with their kids about staying out of trouble and planning their futures.

Aspiring young firefighters frequently visited Station 16, where we all took part in recruiting Black, Latino, and Asian youth into the fire service. We provided mock interviews, shared class information, and informed them about testing opportunities throughout the county. Even during late-night medical calls, two Latina police officers who worked alongside us often acknowledged our positive influence on the neighborhood. I had the pleasure of working with Mexican American colleagues like Henry Mendoza, who had been with me at Station 16 for many years, and later with Ralph Campos and Patricia Tapia.

When Chief Osby left, I felt secure at Station 16 as I served on the executive board of Local 873/230 as the A shift representative. This role allowed me to continue advocating for all firefighters, even though I didn't hold an official rank in the department. I worked hard to establish myself as a leader, but in hindsight, I didn't realize how much my involvement in these extracurricular activities affected my family. I thought I had everything under control, balancing work and home life. I spent countless hours with teachers, doctors, and psychologists and invested a significant amount of money trying to help my oldest daughter, Nicola, navigate her challenges with social interactions. She excelled in math and had a remarkable memory for historical dates, but social situations were difficult for her. It wasn't until Nicola was nearly thirty that she was diagnosed with Autism Spectrum Disorder (ASD). Linda and I had agreed early on that, due to my more flexible work schedule, I would be responsible for attending Nicola's medical and educational appointments.

Girl dad on duty and attending Traci's middle school graduation.

Chapter 11

Racial Estrangement

THIS CHAPTER HIGHLIGHTS PIVOTAL moments in the San Jose Fire Department's history during a period of leadership transitions and systemic challenges. The focus is on Chief Ray Brooks, who faced immense pressure to lead a historically patriarchal and racially divided department through a time of structural and cultural upheaval. His appointment as fire chief marked a new chapter, yet it also unveiled the entrenched resistance to change among some members of the fire department.

The narrative explores the complexities of leadership, from addressing allegations of bias in promotional processes to weathering a controversial no-confidence vote orchestrated by the union. Chief Brooks's efforts to implement merit-based promotions, support diversity, and uphold integrity are juxtaposed against the fierce opposition he encountered. Against this backdrop, the chapter examines the roles of key figures like Regina Williams and the SCCBFA leaders in navigating these tumultuous events, offering a candid lens into the intersection of race, leadership, and institutional accountability.

Fire department chief officers play a vital role in maintaining the stability and effectiveness of the organization. Historically, past San Jose fire chiefs have operated with the approval or guidance of the union and, more recently, the leadership of the department's ethnic and cultural associations. This support was critical because the fire chief oversees the daily operations of a large, historically racist, patriarchal institution. Their responsibilities included providing leadership during emergency incidents, managing the recruitment and training of new personnel, and ensuring that firefighters have the necessary equipment to perform their duties. Between 1992 and 1994, the San Jose Fire Department faced an urgent need to promote several captains to battalion chiefs due to retirements and other departures.

During that same period, Regina Williams became the first Black assistant city manager for the City of San Jose. She had an impressive background and was eager to enhance the fire department's reputation by implementing new city programs. However, Chief Osby, feeling that his management style conflicted with Williams's, left San Jose and pursued a career in San Diego. In his absence, Don Kelly was temporarily promoted to fire chief. Williams then asked City Manager Les White to hire external recruiters to search nationwide for a permanent fire chief before his retirement in 1994. White initially leaned toward hiring a Mexican American fire chief from New Mexico, believing it was necessary to honor the wishes of the Los Bomberos Association, just as he had previously done with the SCCBFA. I thought this decision would benefit the department's diversity, but Local 873/230 opposed it. As a result, White and Williams initiated a second nationwide search.

From the second pool of candidates, White contacted Ray Brooks, the fire chief of Alhambra, California, a small suburban department serving a population of fewer than eighty thousand residents. Brooks had applied during the first search but had not been selected. This time, White offered him the San Jose fire chief position, and Brooks accepted. Williams called Atkinson and me to her office after this decision to discuss the hire. She expressed concerns about Brooks's lack of experience in managing a large fire department and, rather abruptly, remarked that if the hire didn't work out, it would be a problem for the SCCBFA—specifically for Atkinson and me. After the meeting, we discussed her comments, but we were left uncertain about the deeper implications of the assistant city manager's veiled threat.

Lacy Atkinson, president of the SCCBFA, and I reached out to Brooks to welcome him to San Jose. We were excited to have another Black chief in our community and wanted Brooks to feel assured of the SCCBFA's unwavering support. During our conversation, Brooks raised questions about the organization and confidently expressed his qualifications and commitment to excellence. Les White, the former city manager of San Jose, had previously highlighted a critical need for effective leadership, emphasizing that new and younger firefighters required mentors to learn from their successes and failures—a vital part of mastering their craft. Shortly after the job offer, the new city manager, Regina Williams, requested that Chief Brooks promptly fill the vacant captain and battalion chief positions.

We provided Brooks with a list of firefighters who had successfully passed the captain's exam. Among those promoted was Teresa Reed, who made history as the first Black female captain in the county. From the list of captains, Brooks swiftly elevated seven captains to temporary battalion chief positions, the highest front-line rank. While I had mixed feelings about the promotion of Ken Heredia, who was well-supported by many firefighters, I was content when Jerry Williams, a neighbor, was also promoted. However, Jerry's advancement was met with grave resistance from the rank and file. I had suggested several captains I believed were deserving of promotion—individuals I knew would back the new chief—yet their names were overlooked. Instead, Chief Brooks deferred to Chief Osby for the promotional list for battalion chiefs and deputy chiefs. Although there were several battalion chiefs in consideration for the deputy chief position, Brooks faced only one vacancy. He made his decision based on the information available to him at the time, recognizing Battalion Chief Lacy Atkinson for his activism with the SCCBFA and his educational expertise. Brooks promoted Atkinson without hesitation, a choice I considered excellent. While other battalion chiefs had campaigned for the position through union connections, and expressed disappointment at the outcome, Atkinson commanded respect from most union leaders.

To my surprise, Brooks invited me downtown to take on the role of research assistant. My responsibilities included researching new truck and engine equipment to replace outdated gear, as well as conducting diversity training, which garnered widespread acclaim throughout the department as the most effective they had ever experienced.[1] I often met with Chief Brooks to discuss issues related to the union, the SCCBFA, and various matters concerning the fire department. Initially, some employees in the downtown office were upset by my presence, finding my loud voice and straightforward language unsettling. Staying true to myself, I didn't change completely; instead, I adapted by learning to use a computer, organizing meetings, and collaborating with fellow firefighters and secretaries to improve my research reports. This role gave me a new perspective on the fire

---

1. Captain C. Gluck, letter to Chief Staples, Feb. 10, 1995.

department, and I found fulfillment in engaging with paperwork and less physically demanding tasks.

The City of San Jose collaborated with Chief Brooks to hire a consulting firm from Southern California to develop a promotional examination for the battalion chief positions. Brooks understood that he needed an external firm to ensure the promotional process was conducted professionally, legitimately, and transparently. There was no margin for error because battalion chief positions were strictly awarded through a merit-based system, and as the first major decision Brooks would make, the stakes were high.

In May 1995, EDI, the educational organization created by the IAB-PFF, offered classes designed to cultivate leadership skills within the fire service. Firefighters from around the globe attended these summer sessions, which also included preparation for officer examinations. Several San Jose Black firefighters, captains, and officers participated in the workshops. The SCCBFA encouraged all members interested in promotions to captain and battalion chief positions to attend the EDI's May 1995 class. Among the attendees from San Jose were Ray Brooks, Lacy Atkinson, Marvin Coffee, Phil Broussard, Miles Turpin, Jerry Williams, and myself. Fire chief officers from various California cities, including San Francisco and Oakland, delivered presentations that highlighted potential test questions and appropriate answers, sharing insights gleaned from numerous fire department sources, including training programs led by white chief officers.

Throughout the class, participants received thorough instruction and handouts designed to help them understand the roles of department administrators, including various test questions and responses from past exams. Each attendee was issued a large binder to organize their notes and materials—a standard feature of EDI workshops.

Upon returning to his San Jose fire station with his binder, Miles Turpin suggested to his station's crew that he possessed key insights for the upcoming battalion chief exam. He shared his binder with fellow firefighters and extolled the value of the workshops. However, Turpin never explicitly claimed to have a copy of the exam or its answers. Nevertheless, his colleagues quickly assumed that the Black firefighters who attended the EDI classes, under Brooks's leadership, had somehow obtained advanced knowledge of the written test, leading to accusations of cheating. This damaging rumor spread rapidly throughout the department. Once it reached the union, white firefighters intensified the situation by claiming that none of the Black firefighters scheduled to take the exam could possibly succeed without cheating.

In response, Local 873/230 filed a grievance of no confidence against Chief Brooks, attempting to undermine the legitimacy of the exam. An anonymous individual cowardly circulated a letter to union members, urging them to vote "no confidence" in Chief Ray Brooks. This unsigned, defamatory letter targeted every Black firefighter in the department, masquerading as a plea for racial unity.

When Brooks received the notice of the no-confidence vote, he immediately reached out to me, even though I was on a family vacation in New York City. He urged me to return as soon as possible to help defuse the union's actions. Upon my return, I contacted union members to assess the gravity of the situation. Even those I considered allies expressed hostility toward Brooks. Many were irate and unwilling to accept the exam results, accusing Black firefighters of cheating. It remained unclear whether the white firefighters had accurately heard, misinterpreted, or deliberately distorted Miles Turpin's comments. The no-confidence vote was swiftly approved by a majority.

I was furious; I attended the next union meeting with a sense of urgency. I confronted everyone I suspected of harboring anti-Black sentiments, most of whom were present. Drawing on my knowledge of the member's behaviors and tendencies, I addressed their shortcomings—an unexpected move that the union deemed unethical, especially given my role as chair of the Employee Assistance Program (EAP). Local 873/230 accused me of violating confidentiality rules, but I countered that I had only shared information that was already widely known and openly discussed among union members. For instance, I retorted to one member's comment, "Shut up. You are nothing but a drunk anyway." I argued that union meetings should serve as platforms for open dialogue and emphasized that I had not disclosed any confidential information. I also invoked my First Amendment right to free speech during union meetings. Lacy Atkinson attended the meeting to support me, fearing potential violent retaliation from white firefighters in response to my expected remarks.

When the white firefighters realized that many of their colleagues had passed the written exam while only five Black firefighters had succeeded, they became anxious to see the results of the oral board exam. Subsequently, twenty-five of the forty-seven white firefighters failed the oral board exam, and twenty-three of them filed a reverse discrimination lawsuit against the City of San Jose, explicitly targeting Fire Chief Ray Brooks and City Manager Regina Williams. They believed the lawsuit would be an easy win, as several panelists on the oral board were Brooks's colleagues and Black men.

1995 BATTALION CHIEF LIST AS OF JULY 10, 1995

Among the twenty-five white fire captains who failed the oral board exam, twenty-three filed a reverse discrimination lawsuit against Fire Chief Ray Brooks and City Manager Regina Williams.

- Doug Stewart
- John Emmerson
- Don Jonnason
- Mike Jonnason
- Bill Bauer
- Rob Piper
- John Charcho
- Terry Kerns
- Mike Wheaton
- Jim Stunkel
- Dave Moore
- Gary Grenfell
- Dana Reed
- Jim Rozzell
- Bob Gremminger
- Mike Simms
- Stew McGhee
- Steve Felder
- Jim Zubillaga
- Keith Ison
- Mark Mooney
- Keith Keesling
- Greg Spence

In August 1995, a candidate for battalion chief, Captain Robert Gremminger, reported to Deputy Chief Gerald Kohlmann that he had received information about the oral examination questions from Firefighter Miles

Turpin under circumstances that led him to suspect that he (Miles Turpin) might have been given confidential information. Deputy Chief Kohlmann conveyed the report to Chief Brook and Russ Strausbaugh, deputy director of Human Resources. The results were unswerving. Bob Turk, of the City of San Jose Personnel Department, requested a statistical analysis of the battalion chief examination. The study indicated that over the last four battalion chief tests, Black captains who took the examinations had passed in 1984 with 100 percent, in 1987 with 100 percent, in 1991 with 67 percent, and in 1995 with 100 percent. "The Police Department investigation found no evidence that the originally planned questions had been disseminated to anyone not directly involved in the process. Further, the Police Department determined that since the examination was redrafted between 8:30 PM and 4:00 AM the night before the exam began, it was not possible for the oral assessment exam that was used to have been compromised."[2]

On November 2, 1995, Regina Williams demanded that Chief Brooks place me on administrative leave for six months with pay without providing any justification. Williams remained resolute despite Brooks's reluctance and his assertion that I had done nothing wrong and was a good employee. She demanded that Brooks suspend me immediately, insisting that our close relationship must end. I distinctly remember her stating that we (Brooks and I) were "connected at the hip" and that the association needed to cease.

During this poignant time, I attended the Million Man March in Washington, DC. I was inspired by the discourse among Black leaders from across the United States as they shared strategies for advancing social justice. The march helped clarify the extent of my commitment to addressing the injustices fostered by the San Jose Fire Department and the City of San Jose leadership.

The threats to Black firefighters and the community compelled me to file a civil service complaint alleging discrimination. I believed the suspension by Ray Brooks at the behest of Regina Williams was an initial step toward my termination, a pattern I had noticed affecting many Black firefighters over the years. It seemed that white union members and fire department leaders had colluded with Regina Williams.

The coup de grâce was the day after Thanksgiving in 1995 when Regina Williams fired Brooks. Brooks later sued the City of San Jose for wrongful

---

2. Donnoe & Associates, "Battalion Chief Results" letter to Bob Turk, City of San Jose, Aug. 22, 1995.

termination and won. He became the fire chief in Birmingham, Alabama, and later served as the assistant city manager of Compton, California.

MY CIVIL SERVICE COMMISSION HEARINGS

When I submitted my complaint to the civil service commissioners, I couldn't help but contemplate who among my acquaintances might influence the commission's decision, for better or worse. One of my long-standing adversaries, John Diquisto, a union leader with years of service on Local 873/230, came to mind. Diquisto and I had clashed numerous times, particularly during my younger, more confrontational days. I had often felt wronged by the white leadership of the union, which led to my frequent defiance of Diquisto. After retiring as captain from the San Jose Fire Department, Diquisto entered politics and was elected to the San Jose City Council. Diquisto's influence reached beyond the fire department; it was known that he had established connections with Dutch Hammer, a prior city manager who held the position for some nineteen years and who was a notable figure in local Elks and Masons organizations. Diquisto's network included the Civil Service Commission and the San Jose Fire Department. He also attracted the attention of the newly appointed City Manager, Regina Williams, as she sought to establish her authority in her new role. I was concerned that Diquisto and Williams might have influence with the Civil Service Commission and negatively influence my career.

After the dismissal of Chief Ray Brooks, Regina Williams appointed Robert Dorman as the acting San Jose fire chief. Dorman, a veteran battalion chief with thirty-one years of experience, was well-liked by the union, providing Regina Williams with a convenient shield against any criticism directed at her leadership. *Mercury News* had reported that Dorman admitted to privately meeting with several white captains for lunch in December 1995, after becoming fire chief and during the time that their reverse discrimination lawsuit was still pending.

The Notice of Intended Discipline (NOID) against me issued by Chief Robert Dorman included two main charges: (1) Misconduct involving failure to satisfactorily perform the duties of the position, neglecting to observe applicable rules and regulations, and being discourteous to other employees, along with other actions deemed detrimental to public service. (2) Alleged misconduct and discourteous treatment of a public member during an off-duty public meeting.

During five months of Civil Service Commission hearings, my reputation was severely attacked, with numerous accusations regarding events that had never been litigated within the fire department or the courts. Regina Williams expressed her desire for the hearings to illustrate that I had a pattern of behavior unworthy of a firefighter. With the reluctant support of various firefighters, both Black and white, several alleged transgressions over my twenty-plus years in the fire service were scrutinized. While many of my African American friends stood by me throughout the hearings, a white colleague, Captain Bobby Wells, who had worked alongside me for years, refused to testify against me despite intense pressure from the city and the union. I was wrongfully accused of exposing a sexual incident between two firefighters that occurred at Station 16—an event I was not involved in, though I was aware of the rumors circulating at the time.

Fire Engineer Henry Mendoza, a Latino man I had worked with for many years and a family friend, also declined to testify against me despite duress from the city and the Los Bomberos. It remains unclear what they wanted from Mendoza, as we were friends, and to my memory, I had done nothing wrong during our time working together. Furthermore, both Wells and Mendoza were pressured to identify incidents from many years past that were unrelated to the current allegations. Captain Richard Santos, a friend, union leader, and confidant, attended every hearing, offering words of encouragement and sharing insights about the San Jose Fire Department's and the union's strategies. Notably, Chief Robert Osby traveled nearly four hundred miles from San Diego to San Jose to serve as a supportive witness, providing a strong endorsement of my character.

The city's attorney challenged Osby's testimony by referencing an incident from my past. Osby responded deliberately, stating, "The other person was not credible." He described me as an honest, deeply committed, and emotional Black man who had dedicated his life to combating anti-Black racism and the micro- and macroaggressions that dehumanize Black men. Osby characterized me as a warrior, a man of my word. Many individuals rallied around Linda and me, contributing funds and supporting us emotionally. Several Black firefighters regularly took us out for lunch or dinner to lift our spirits. Deputy Chief Atkinson served as my friend, confidant, and spiritual advisor throughout the civil service hearings, helping my family navigate the barrage of hateful news articles and vitriol from white firefighters. Atkinson's friendship was important because he had the indelible trust of the fire department, union, and community as an honorable man.

My attorney, Allen Ruby of the Law Offices of Ruby & Schofield law firm, was most crucial to my defense. A well-respected lawyer in the South Bay and Bay Area, Ruby dedicated countless hours discussing the San Jose Fire Department with me and expressed his belief that the department had become corruptly racist. He was unapologetic in voicing his opinion. Ruby effectively challenged many of the accusations that were irrelevant to the reasons for my discipline but were nonetheless used to construct a damaging narrative against me. He pointed out that white firefighters who used similar language and forceful actions were not disciplined, with several receiving promotions. At one point, Fire Chief Dorman admitted that a white firefighter's alleged shooting of a Black man in a mall parking lot was a single incident worse than anything I had done. Yet, Dorman deemed my conduct over an extended period to be the worst he had ever encountered. Ruby concluded the session by highlighting Dorman's inarticulate and racist statements.

Ruby was encouraging, supportive, and always available. He felt that using false actions and statements was Regina Williams's only chance of getting rid of me. Some of the accusations expressed words that I had never used against anyone, words like "honkies" and "rednecks," words that were never a part of my lexicon. White firefighters overstated several violent events to justify their accusations. Regina Williams was willing to do anything to keep her position and show the union and the city leadership she was in control.

One of my closest friends and colleagues, Jesse Savage, gave a riveting interview to the San Jose *Mercury News* about the racism in the fire department. The article reflected a former US Army veteran's experience after joining the San Jose Fire Department in 1976. He had initially viewed the department as a close-knit community dedicated to public safety but soon encountered systemic domination and abuse reminiscent of past oppressive environments. He perceived ongoing racial tensions, with visible animosity from white firefighters, fear among Black firefighters, and division among minority groups. More recently, he had criticized the unfair firing of Fire Chief Ray Brooks and accusations against Black firefighters, which he viewed as unjust and racially motivated. He expressed particular concern over the dehumanization and slander I had experienced, praising my supportive nature. The veteran cited two independent consultants confirming racism within the department and believed the city administration had contributed to creating a racist environment.

At the end of the hearings, the civil service commissioners convened to discuss the case and determine the final consequences. Several representatives on the commission advocated for my termination and the denial of my pension. However, one commissioner, a proud Latino man, stood firmly against firing me. He argued that I deserved the right to retire after serving as a stellar firefighter for twenty-plus years. He was resolute in his position, insisting that everyone must stay in the meeting until an agreement to allow retirement was reached. This commissioner was well-informed about systemic racism and the adverse conditions created by militaristic organizations such as the fire department. He advocated for social justice during the struggles in East Side San Jose in the 1970s and 1980s.

While the suspension was not overturned entirely, the terms of the discipline were reduced. Several accusations were debunked, and all allegations made before January 8, 1993, were excluded from the charges. The financial penalties were decreased from a twenty-six-week suspension and salary reduction to an eighteen-week suspension and salary reduction over nine pay periods. Zeke Garcia concurred with some opinions but wanted the suspension removed and the pay reduction decreased by two additional weeks.[3]

The Eligibility Report for the battalion chief position was developed during my suspension but sent out to the public on November 27, 1996, causing many ill feelings among the white firefighters.

Ranking order

- Floyd D. Stewart
- Dana C. Reed
- James C. Stunkel
- Robert H. Piper
- William R. Bauer
- Donald C. Jonnason
- Randall L. Courts
- Michael T. Jonnason
- Stewart A. McGhee
- John W. Emmerson

3. Witt, "Firefighter's Discipline."

- Thomas H. Afflixio

- Michael A. Wheaton

- Gregory D. Spence

- Terry L. Kerns

- John T. Charcho

- James W. Zubillaga

- Michael E. Simms

- Charles J. Gluck

- Philip Broussard

- Robert B. King

- Marvin M. Coffee

- Robert R. Reeks

- Mark B. Mooney

- Oscar J. Martinez Jr.

- Jerry Williams

Two Black firefighters had been promoted before posting the final battalion chief eligibility list: Chief Raymond Brooks promoted Lacy Atkinson to deputy chief and Chief Dorman promoted Nick Thomas to battalion chief.

While suspended, I consulted with Allen Ruby, my attorney, to discuss the possibility of suing the San Jose Fire Department for discrimination. Once the disciplinary period was over, I requested to return to work at Station 25, where Marvin Coffee was the captain and Melvin Meeks was the battalion chief. Meeks was a Black man promoted by Chief Osby and someone I had worked with during our early careers when Meeks was a fire engineer. I knew Meeks was angry because he had also applied for the deputy chief position awarded to Chief Atkinson, but my naivety interfered with any suspicion of hatred. During the civil service hearing, it became clear that Meeks hated me. A level of hatred I hope never to understand.

RACIAL ESTRANGEMENT

"Anybody who teaches Negros today to turn the other cheek is eventually committing a crime. Anyone who teaches the Negro to

love those who hate him is making the Negro go contrary to the law of nature and making the Negro go contrary to his intelligence."
—Trusty's mantra—from the teachings of Malcomb X

Chapter 12

San Jose Fire Captain

San Jose Fire Captain Kills a Black Man

THIS CHAPTER EXPLORES A tumultuous period in Trusty's career, marked by relentless adversity and a hard-fought path toward resolution. After returning to the fire service following the Civil Service Commission decision, he sought refuge in the camaraderie of trusted allies, such as Captain Marvin Coffee. However, his hope for a peaceful working environment was quickly upended by the antagonism of Engineer Terry Meinzer, whose actions underscored the enduring challenges of navigating a hostile workplace steeped in racial bias. The struggle escalated, forcing Trusty to confront not only professional sabotage efforts from the battalion chief but also personal decisions about his future in the fire service.

Through the lens of his battle for disability retirement, this chapter illustrates the systemic inequities within the fire department's rules for retirement and broader societal forces at play. From facing dismissive psychiatrists to pushing through bureaucratic resistance, Trusty was determined to claim the benefits long denied to Black firefighters. The events surrounding the SCCBFA during this time—including the fallout from a shocking act of violence committed by a former San Jose fire captain—highlighted the deep divisions within their ranks and the community. Together, these experiences shaped Dudley's final steps in a career defined by an unwavering commitment to social justice.

After being reinstated as a firefighter, I requested a transfer to Station 25, where Fire Captain Marvin Coffee, my true friend and brother, was in charge. However, instead of finding a calm and safe environment, I became a target for the station's engineer, Terry Meinzer. He immediately tested my patience, believing that the civil service hearings had shaken my confidence. Fire Engineer Terry Meinzer, a young white man eager for promotion, relentlessly targeted me with verbal assaults. He made a concerted effort to provoke arguments and create conflict at the station. Meinzer informed Battalion Chief Meeks about our discussions and sent him several memos complaining about me. In response, Captain Coffee addressed the memos to Chief Meeks, explaining that Meinzer should not override his responsibility as my immediate supervisor by continually sending messages to the battalion chief and by trying to provoke me into arguments, hoping I would react in a way that would lead to my dismissal. However, Meeks agreed with Meinzer and blamed Coffee and me for the disturbances. Ultimately Meinzer became a captain for a short time.

To escape the worsening situation, I transferred to Station 5 where another friend and supporter, Captain Dick Santo, led the crew. I was assigned to Truck 5. It was during this time that I began seriously planning for retirement, although I hadn't yet completed the required twenty-five years of full-time service—I still needed two more years because the two years working under the CETA (Comprehensive Employment and Training Act) program didn't count toward that total. To secure a disability retirement pension, I required an indisputable claim that the union couldn't challenge, as they were set on denying me the benefits. They'd rather see me shoulder the total tax burden than allow me to access the tax breaks that come with a disability retirement. This retirement benefit was awarded to many white firefighters. The tax benefit amount associated with disability retirement is determined by the severity of one's physical or mental condition. Firefighters do not receive Social Security benefits.

I initially filed for disability retirement based on Post-Traumatic Stress Disorder (PTSD), linking it to the racism and discrimination I faced as a Black firefighter in the San Jose Fire Department. In my request, I cited a specific incident that occurred on October 24, 1996, when a white San Jose Fire Department captain, Robert Gremminger, shot and killed a young Black man in a shopping mall parking lot in Milpitas, California. This incident deeply outraged me and underscored the anti-Black racism within the department. Before Gremminger killed the Black man, I had confronted him over his boasting about violent encounters and his methods of overpowering Black men during his career as a police officer. I challenged him, daring him to try to overpower me. When he didn't respond, I left the station.[1]

The SCCBFA felt betrayed by some white colleagues who stood by Gremminger. Many Black firefighters were enraged by the leniency of his sentencing. It was a tense period for everyone, with white firefighters expressing a range of emotions—shock, shame, and anger—over the nine years sentencing Gremminger received.

> Robert Gremminger, at 56, hung his head as a jury convicted him of involuntary manslaughter. Santa Clara County prosecutor Joyce Allegro remarked that Gremminger carried an unlicensed loaded revolver into a crowded shopping center, firing it into the parking lot. Allegro stated that Gremminger claimed he needed the gun for protection against Black San Jose firefighters due to threats he had received related to a lawsuit. Gremminger had been a central figure in a failed reverse discrimination lawsuit that accused Black firefighters of cheating on a promotion exam.[2]

Gremminger ultimately served seven years of a nine-year sentence for killing thirty-year-old Anthony Gilbert at the Milpitas Great Mall, a location that had once been a Ford manufacturing plant—my first employer when I moved to San Jose. The incident was horrifying, and many African Americans in Northern California, particularly Black firefighters, were outraged by the lenient sentence. Despite this, Gremminger managed to secure a service retirement, aided by several chief officers, including a Black battalion chief. This event had long-lasting repercussions for Black firefighters across the county. Gremminger was also one of the prominent figures accusing Black firefighters of cheating on the 1995 battalion chief exam. While citizen protests demanded that he receive a sentence fitting the crime, Local 873/230 and many city employees rallied behind him, advocating for no jail time.

Realizing the inevitable consequences of remaining a San Jose firefighter, I decided to act quickly and file for retirement. I sought help from Jim Jeffers, a retirement and workers' compensation attorney who had successfully assisted many firefighters of color with their retirement applications. However, Jim was cautious about my PTSD claim. He warned me that a mental health diagnosis might affect my future job prospects. I

---

1. Santos, personal communication, Feb. 4, 2024.
2. Finz, "Ex-Fireman Sentenced." See also Gonzales, "Gremminger Bail."

explained that I was experiencing the classic symptoms of PTSD, repeatedly reliving the trauma of the severe institutional and structural racism I had endured throughout my career. The injustices highlighted during my civil service hearing triggered painful memories and flashbacks. I wasn't looking for another job—I was ready to rely on my current resources. In Santa Clara County, most attorneys avoided taking cases for Black firefighters, likely because many had close ties with Local 873/230. No firefighter had ever filed a PTSD-related disability retirement claim based on racism in the San Jose Fire Department. Despite his concerns, Jim Jeffers was an invaluable ally, helping me complete the paperwork and connecting me with local psychiatrists.

Unfortunately, I faced significant resistance. Three psychiatrists seemed determined to reject my disability claim. I discovered that Local 873/230 was monitoring my psychiatric visits, intent on blocking my access to the benefits I rightfully deserved. In total, I consulted with four psychiatrists before my disability retirement was finally approved.

The first psychologist dismissed me, claiming I was "dressed too well" to be suffering from PTSD. He acknowledged that PTSD is a mental disorder linked to traumatic experiences but insisted that my situation didn't fit the legal definition. Other psychologists stated that I was too intelligent and articulate to qualify for disability, suggesting PTSD wasn't a recognized condition in the fire service. They even asserted that too many firefighters were receiving disability retirements, and they felt that using PTSD as a claim was unfair to the department. The last psychiatrist, however, a young Mexican American, didn't even get the chance to assess me. When I walked into his office, I was blunt and told him that if I faced another racist incident at a fire station, I would harm someone like him. Without hesitation, he signed off on my disability retirement and insisted I leave his office immediately.

Although my condition wasn't officially labeled as PTSD, I was diagnosed with a mental stress illness that still qualified me for disability retirement. At that point, I didn't care what the diagnosis was called; I just wanted the same disability retirement that many white firefighters had been granted. However, it took two years before I started receiving the payments. Eventually, I was approved for an 80 percent disability retirement, which meant I wouldn't have to pay taxes on 80 percent of my pension.

This ordeal seriously tested my resolve. I questioned why I had to resort to threats or outbursts of anger toward people of the dominant culture to receive equal treatment. My friends expressed concern about my diagnosis, but I was exhausted from the psychological evaluations' delays and was eager to complete the retirement process so that I could focus on other aspects of my life.

SCCBFA'S DILEMMA

The SCCBFA faced challenges with the African American community, as many leaders felt caught between supporting Chief Brooks and Regina Williams. Media coverage, particularly by the *Monterey Herald*, appeared to favor Williams. After Chief Brooks was dismissed, the NAACP informed me that they supported Williams and the Black firefighters who had passed the exam. The NAACP's president, and an African American woman, made it clear that the organization was backing Williams, the first Black woman to serve as San Jose's city manager.

At that time, I found myself home alone, isolated from friends and peers. I had never anticipated losing the civil service hearing and was left to aggrieve everything that had unfolded. Once my retirement paperwork was finalized, I was no longer part of the fire service. My family was supportive but concerned about my well-being. Nicola and Traci were living independently: Traci was married for the second time and residing in Fremont, California, while Nicola was still single and living in Santa Clara. Linda had accepted a substantial buyout from Pacific Bell in the same month I retired, and we began discussing our lives after the fire department. However, I grew increasingly worried about the SCCBFA. The association was losing the sponsorship from the Black community for the first time, feeling disrespected and dishonored due to the civil service hearing loss and the reverse discrimination lawsuit that accused Ray Brooks and Black firefighters of cheating on a battalion chief exam.

White firefighters deemed Regina Williams, the first Black city manager, unfit for her job simply because she hired Ray Brooks. Her position became precarious; in her desperate bid to maintain her job, she aligned herself with white firefighters intent on erasing my career achievements and tarnishing my reputation with community leaders.

Several Black community leaders confided in me about their dilemma. Regina had communicated her stance to the African American organizations in San Jose. They were torn between continuing their support for the Black firefighters, whom they had respected and honored for many years, or siding with Regina Williams, the first Black woman in such a prominent role. Organizations such as the NAACP, Black educators, Black police associations, and local churches chose to support Williams, prioritizing her position over the people. These groups represented the African American upper middle class: well-educated professionals who often aligned themselves with white organizations throughout Santa Clara County—organizations that supported white firefighters.

However, smaller and less influential Black organizations affiliated with the city's leaders (including community-based businesses and barbershops), restaurant owners, and working-class individuals continued to back the Black firefighters. This division revealed the complexities of a caste system in our Black community—a tactic used to undermine and discredit the accomplishments of Black people.

But the white firefighters failed in their reverse discrimination lawsuit—the court found no evidence of wrongdoing. White firefighters' reputations suffered as well, as numerous accusations and evidence of racism came to light, mainly several acts against communities of color. White firefighters had to confront the uncomfortable fact that one of their own, a leader who loathed Black men, had been convicted of the senseless murder of a young Black citizen from Oakland. During the murder trial, several white firefighters admitted to their racist actions against Black individuals. At the time, however, they were unaware that their actions were both racist and discriminatory towards me and other Black firefighters. The prevailing mantra among the white San Jose firefighters was, "It was always Bynoe's fault."

Chapter 13

They Were My Brothers

IN THE MID-1990S, THE tides of civil rights battles shifted dramatically, with federal courts inundated by a surge of cases addressing systemic discrimination. For the SCCBFA and its allies, this era epitomized both the urgency and complexity of their struggle for equity. Against a backdrop of deep-seated racism and institutional resistance, Trusty spearheaded a federal civil rights lawsuit aimed at confronting discriminatory practices within the San Jose Fire Department. This chapter captures the meticulous preparation, strategic alliances, and unyielding resilience that defined this pivotal legal fight, even as it exposed fractures within the SCCBFA and the broader Black community.

The stakes could not have been higher. For Trusty and his coplaintiffs, this case was not just about individual justice but about affirming the humanity and worth of every Black firefighter who had endured systemic discrimination. Despite the overwhelming odds, Trusty approached this challenge with unwavering determination, blending legal strategy with grassroots solidarity. As the trial unfolded, the courtroom became a battleground where truths about institutional racism were laid bare, and the limits of justice were tested. This chapter vividly details the personal sacrifices, legal maneuvers, and collective efforts that marked this historic fight for social justice.

After the expansion of civil rights laws in the early 1990s, the number of civil rights cases filed in US district courts rose significantly, increasing from 18,922 in 1990 to 43,278 in 1997. From 1996 to 1997, jury trials became more prevalent than bench trials; however, the percentage of plaintiffs who won their trials remained around 33 percent.[1] Despite knowing the odds were against us, I remained hopeful that we could achieve a victory. Throughout the 1990s, civil rights claims increasingly dominated the federal caseloads in US district courts. My concern was the division within the Black community, and I felt a deep obligation to restore honor to the SCCBFA. I had promised the SCCBFA that I would do everything in my power to prevent any lasting harm, but I knew I couldn't achieve this alone.

I had already been in the fight of my life; the Civil Service Commission had reached its final decision. The newly appointed fire chief, Robert Dorman, wanted to fire me. At the same time, Regina Williams sought to teach me a lesson for being vocal and standing up to the department leader's blatant racist attitudes. In February 1996, Williams and Dorman promoted thirteen captains to battalion chief. The three Black captains—Williams, Coffee, and Broussard—were not considered for promotion. I asked Ruby to consider filing a federal discrimination lawsuit with multiple plaintiffs. I proposed he included: Jerry Williams, Marvin Coffee, and Phil Broussard.

Ruby considered my suggestion and explored the possibility of including a white battalion chief candidate who the union and the San Jose Fire Department had rejected. Ruby believed that our case would be stronger if we could demonstrate that the San Jose Fire Department and the City of San Jose were not only racist against Black men but also unjustly wielded their power against anyone, including white men, who didn't conform to the "good ole boys" network. This network empowered white firefighters while limiting opportunities for Black firefighters. I recommended Randy Courts, a fair open-minded white man who had supported me throughout my career. Ruby liked the idea of including Courts because he had ranked among the top ten highest scorers on the battalion chief exam. Courts could corroborate the institution's racist practices and actions. He epitomized how white firefighters would be discriminated against when they associated with or supported Black firefighters and the SCCBFA. Courts had been ousted from the "good ole boys" club for years because of unfounded accusations and his friendship with me. When I talked with Courts, he

---

1. Kyckelhahn and Cohen, "Civil Rights Complaints."

agreed to join the lawsuit and pledged to do whatever he could to support a positive outcome.

Ruby insinuated that I had the stronger case; my employment was suspended without cause or validity. He believed my case was more winnable than those of the four fire captains who had passed a promotion exam but were overlooked, especially since twenty-five white fire captains were also not promoted. Ruby considered the variables involved in scoring the fire department exams, which included a promotional test consisting of a written exam and an oral assessment interview based on the position. My case centered on the San Jose Fire Department condemning and punishing me for alleged past discretions unrelated to the current accusations that had never been prosecuted. Additionally, Ruby believed I could overturn the Civil Service Commission ruling because I had only discussed well-known information with union members at a union meeting and had not divulged any personal information obtained as the EAP chair. Ruby proposed that I had free speech rights in the union meeting as determined by Local 875/230 rules.

While Ruby was confident that I had the stronger case, I felt it was essential to ensure that the brothers on the battalion chief list received justice. I insisted that the lawsuit benefit all the firefighters affected by the actions of certain white union members who conducted a no-confidence vote against Chief Ray Brooks. This included the twenty-three promotion-eligible fire captains who had filed a reverse discrimination suit against the San Jose Fire Department and the City of San Jose, alleging that Chief Ray Brooks and the SCCBFA had cheated on the battalion chief exams.

The Black firefighters needed to understand I was not solely focused on my well-being. Many SCCBFA members were like family to me. We traveled across the country together, attended conferences and conventions, and spoke out against the racist and sexist actions of various fire departments. They were my brothers; you never leave your brothers behind, and I believed they always had my back. We even had nicknames for one another; I was known as Trusty the Crazy Bajan, a man of his word.

Ruby agreed to file a civil rights case in the San Jose Federal Court, but only if he could collaborate with another law firm due to the extensive number of depositions and the level of work involved. He partnered with William Chapman from the Chapman, Popik, & White law firm, and requested fifty thousand dollars to begin the depositions. I reached out to the three Black captains on the promotional list—Coffee, Broussard, and

Williams—to gauge their interest in joining a federal lawsuit against the City of San Jose and the San Jose Fire Department.

Chief Dorman's appointment as fire chief was based on the city manager's expectation that he could transform the troubled fire department into a more civil, conciliatory, and inclusive organization.[2] The San Jose Fire Department had faced significant issues related to racism and favoritism and had barely survived several legal challenges. Chief Dorman interviewed the three Black captains, and it became evident from the nature of his questions and demeanor that they would not be receiving promotions. Marvin Coffee noted that Dorman's interview questions for the battalion chief position were extreme and disrespectful. Dorman questioned Coffee's loyalty to Brooks and the Local 873/230, asking whether he could instead be loyal to him.

As expected, Coffee, Williams, and Broussard were not promoted to battalion chief. Coffee and Broussard agreed immediately to join the civil rights lawsuit; Williams, however, was hesitant. Having served as a temporary battalion chief for several months, he believed he might eventually be promoted permanently. Additionally, he was concerned that my civil service hearing could negatively impact his chances for promotion. Ruby's "Contingency Fee Agreement for the Civil Rights Lawsuit Against the City of San Jose," dated May 29, 1996, required the plaintiffs to agree to the binding effect of the decision. Williams ultimately joined the lawsuit. This was Ruby's agreement:

> Binding Effect of Decisions by Other Plaintiffs. The lawsuit will be a joint undertaking among all of you, in which the success or failure of each of you is tied to the success or failure of the group. For that reason, you need to agree on terms that tie you together for the duration of the lawsuit. I cannot impose such an agreement upon you. However, I feel so strongly about the need for it that I am only willing to proceed as your attorney if you mutually commit to the others.[3]

According to their bylaws, union leaders were obligated to fund members' court cases, as most members paid dues throughout their careers. I had paid dues for twenty years, and all the other plaintiffs had done the same. However, Local 873/230 was far from equitable in distributing their support and funds. For instance, the union hall was utilized to meet, plan,

2. Romano, "Fire Chief Gets Credit."
3. Ruby, letter to Coffee, Williams, Broussard, and Bynoe, May 29, 1996.

and gather information for the no-confidence vote against Chief Brooks and the reverse discrimination lawsuit against Brooks, Regina Williams, and the SCCBFA, which had accused them of cheating on the battalion chief exam.

Additionally, Local 873/230 rules stipulated that they could not file suits against union members. Nonetheless, they utilized members' money to undermine Chief Brooks's credibility and to file a reverse discrimination suit against Black firefighters. The union also took extensive measures to conceal the identities of the twenty-three white firefighters who filed the reverse discrimination charges. The distribution of funds by the union was blatantly unfair, with white firefighters receiving twenty-five thousand dollars for their legal fees while Black firefighters were allocated only twenty-five hundred dollars. In contrast, the SCCBFA supported the Black firefighters by covering the initial fifty thousand dollar payment requested by Ruby and Chapman. Many Black firefighter organizations nationwide helped finance our lawsuit.

Tommy Fulcher, the CEO of Economic Social Opportunity, played a vital role in supporting the SCCBFA by hosting successful fundraising events at his home in downtown San Jose. I still recall when Teresa Deloach Reed became the first SCCBFA member to make a significant financial contribution to our cause. My commitment to raising funds and ensuring our legal bills were paid on time never wavered. When the newly appointed SCCBFA president failed to settle several attorney bills promptly, I intervened, even though I didn't hold an official position at the time. I had always emphasized the importance of paying attorney bills upon receipt to maintain a respectful attorney-client relationship. Acting swiftly, I removed the current president and appointed Kevin Taylor as the new SCCBFA president for the duration of the trial. Having worked closely with Taylor before, I trusted his dedication to the SCCBFA and me. While this resolved the immediate issue, other disruptive behaviors continued to create problems behind the scenes.

I attended every deposition, observing as white firefighters squirmed under the probing questions from Ruby and Chapman. Marvin Coffee and Randy Courts often joined me during these sessions. When jury selection began, one potential juror caught our attention: a Black woman who had previously worked for Santa Clara County. Initially, we believed her presence on the jury would be advantageous. Unfortunately, she turned out to be an infiltrator for the city, intent on undermining the jury's sympathy for

Black firefighters. Ethel Williams, the wife of Jerry Williams, was the only member of our team who expressed doubts about this young Black woman, questioning her eagerness to serve on the jury.

I was pleased with the other jurors; they appeared younger and professional, intelligent, and knowledgeable about workplace issues, including both explicit and implicit racism. In many trials I've observed, jurors often consisted of older white individuals who were uninformed about the experiences of Black people and the realities of institutional racism.

The trial in Chief Magistrate Judge Edward Infante's San Jose courtroom was slated for six weeks. The plaintiffs decided on a dress code, wearing dark suits and white shirts and sitting in the front row to carefully observe the proceedings. Once the jury was selected, the trial kicked off on July 28, 1998. In his opening statement, Ruby outlined the racist aggression Black firefighters in San Jose endured while striving to provide equal service to the citizens in their communities. As Ruby declared, "The plaintiffs always wanted to be treated just like everybody else, and they were in court because they weren't treated like everybody else."[4]

This opening statement vividly illustrated the racism embedded in many militaristic and patriarchal environments, highlighting how systemic anti-Black racism marginalizes Black individuals. Ruby pointed out that when faced with a large, vocal Black man, white individuals often resort to labeling him a monster out of fear. Despite recognizing the deep-seated nature of the racism we were addressing, the impact of the opening statements left us feeling optimistic.

Conversely, the city attorneys depicted the plaintiffs as individuals seeking undue advantage due to their association with a Black fire chief who allegedly provided them with unearned opportunities. Their strategy involved attacking my character, which had previously been effective during the civil service hearing. However, this time, Ruby and Chapman successfully blocked any mention of unsubstantiated past actions irrelevant to our case. Unfortunately, similar derogatory tactics were used to undermine Broussard, Coffee, Courts, and Williams.

Ruby and Chapman effectively demonstrated that other firefighters and captains shared similar experiences, which were resolved through proper documentation. Ruby highlighted that several firefighters on the battalion chief list had similar transgressions, yet their incidents did not disqualify them from consideration for the battalion chief position.

4. Witt, "Trial of Fire Chief."

Each plaintiff gave professional testimony detailing the anti-Black racism they faced throughout their careers. Some stories were deeply moving, revealing how white firefighters mishandled the homes of people of color and spoke disrespectfully to residents from those communities. All plaintiffs confirmed these accounts, sharing instances of racist, sexist, and vile language, along with acts of physical aggression directed at them and others in their fire stations.

Interestingly, some white firefighters admitted, under cross-examination, that they learned a great deal from working with me and wouldn't have had such an understanding of people of color's experiences without our interactions. One firefighter even noted he had learned to accept being called "motherfucker" while speaking with me yet acknowledged his respect for my professionalism as a firefighter and union representative.

Melvin Meeks and Lacy Atkinson testified on behalf of the San Jose Fire Department. Meeks displayed apparent hostility toward each Black plaintiff, especially toward me, due to feeling slighted and disrespected at some point in our relationship. In contrast, Atkinson testified because he was one of three chiefs involved in assessing and scoring the plaintiffs during their oral exams. The other panel members included Chief Dorman and Assistant Chief Bruce Staples. The defense attorney strategically called Atkinson as a witness to exploit racial dynamics for their benefit, essentially playing the "race game." However, this tactic inadvertently strengthened the plaintiffs' case, as Atkinson's actions and statements throughout the trial ultimately supported us.

The federal trial audience differed from those at the Civil Service Commission hearings. The federal court sessions took place over several weeks, running Tuesday to Thursday, while the civil service hearings were held in the evenings over several months to accommodate witnesses and supporters. My civil service hearing was one of the longest, if not *the* longest, hearings in the history of the Civil Service Commission in San Jose.

Ray Brooks frequently attended federal court sessions, usually sitting alone. Throughout the trial, Black firefighters and their families showed unwavering support. Coffee's siblings, Ethel Williams and Sharon Broussard, were regular attendees. Meanwhile, very few white firefighters came to support Courts, although his wife's attendance was limited due to the long commute from Yosemite. Linda was present daily, sitting directly behind us and providing positive support in an intense atmosphere. I felt proud of my fellow plaintiffs as they spoke with strength, fully aware that this was the most important battle of their careers.

The court unanimously received documents from the San Jose Fire Department that aided our case, and Coffee provided evidence supporting our allegations against Dorman. Ruby considered me a natural storyteller, allowing my storyline to emphasize the injustice of the defendants' claims.

Despite our efforts, the verdict came back with eight votes in favor of us and three against, leading to a victory for the City of San Jose. The outcome devastated me; I feared we had lost our last chance to effect lasting change within the department's system. I withdrew, consumed by anger and sadness, until my best friend and confidant, Carl Lacey, intervened. He reminded me that fighting the city was like challenging one of the most entrenched white power structures in the nation, emphasizing that white firefighters were universally loved.

Carl shared that when Black individuals challenge white militaristic patriarchal systems, they must anticipate rule changes, accept lies and claims of victimhood used both to maintain power and demean those they consider "inferior." He recounted historical struggles lost over time, beginning with Native peoples and treaties continually violated to dispossess them of their land, marking the birth of practices designed to marginalize other groups. Despite the loss, Carl expressed immense pride in my strength and courage to confront such power. He suggested that a victory for Black firefighters could have sparked significant change in the country and that San Jose wasn't ready to be held responsible for it.

The next day, Ruby called to set up an appointment. Surprisingly, Ruby seemed pleased with the eight-three verdict, believing it showed potential for further action. Though I hadn't expected his optimism, I was excited to hear his thoughts.

Chapter 14

Bringing Mr. Turner Home

IN THIS CHAPTER, THE emotional weight of both public and personal struggles takes center stage. The fallout from losing the civil service hearing against the San Jose Fire Department intensifies as Trusty navigates the turmoil of a discrimination trial in federal court. Against the backdrop of systemic racism and hostility within the fire service, Trusty and his colleagues fight to expose and challenge the deep-rooted inequities in their profession. Amid these legal battles, personal crises arise as Trusty and his wife, Linda, confront the devastating illness of her father, Mr. Turner, forcing them to reimagine their lives beyond San Jose.

Through a brief respite in Hilton Head, South Carolina, Trusty begins to rediscover himself, only to be pulled back into the harsh realities of caregiving and a second federal trial. With Linda's determination to protect her family and Trusty's resolve to rebuild in Monterey, their journey becomes one of resilience and transformation. This chapter captures the intersection of systemic challenges and personal renewal, as Trusty learns to channel his advocacy and purpose into a new community while processing the setbacks and lessons from his fight for justice.

After losing the civil service hearing against the San Jose Fire Department, my life was chaotic, marked by family turmoil and legal battles. The discrimination trial occurred in the US District Court in San Jose, presided over by Chief Magistrate Judge Edward Infante. It felt like a relentless storm. My colleagues—Coffee, Broussard, Williams, and Courts—claimed their careers had been sabotaged by the entrenched "good ole boys" network, which was intent on denying them opportunities for promotions. I had fought for my rights, my freedom of speech, and the courage to stand against a workplace steeped in toxic, anti-Black hostility. But there are always problems lurking in the background. In this chapter, the trouble was the serious illness afflicting Linda's father. It would change the trajectory of my life.

Desperate for an escape, Linda and I decided to trade the oppressive atmosphere of San Jose for a different kind of environment. We joined Tommy Fulcher and his family, along with Ray Brooks and his wife, Paulette, for a vacation in Hilton Head, South Carolina. This trip was a breath of fresh air, a much-needed reprieve that began transforming my mindset. I found it curious that all the resort properties were named after southern plantations, yet I couldn't help but enjoy the stunning golf courses, the inviting pools, and the thrill of parasailing. Linda and I took golf lessons and played our first game together. Our golf swings may have been abysmal, but the shared laughs, challenges, and island experiences drew me into the sport, igniting a passion I didn't know I had.

While we explored the islands of South Carolina, we connected with the descendants of enslaved individuals who once toiled in the rice fields. Their stories of resilience and transformation—from enslaved fishermen to small business owners to farmers—were both inspiring and heartbreaking. Yet it was tragic to learn how questionable federal tax laws and heritage scams had stripped them of thousands of acres of land in the mid-1900s.

TAKING CARE OF MR. TURNER

Our time in Hilton Head was abruptly interrupted by devastating news: Linda's father was gravely ill, diagnosed with stage four lung cancer. We hurried back to San Jose, where Linda stepped into the role of primary caregiver. She arranged for him to be treated at the Stanford Medical Center, where doctors confirmed that Mr. Turner's cancer had already metastasized to his brain, giving him mere months to live.

Faced with this harsh reality, Mr. Turner expressed a desire to be closer to his wife—Linda's mother—and his other daughters, Lilyette and Leza. This revelation motivated Linda to consider a move for our family. She was deeply worried about my mental health; the anger and pain I felt were hard to mask, and San Jose had become a hostile environment. Old wounds ran deep, and I found myself at odds with certain firefighters—particularly Melvin Meeks, Gremminger, and several union leaders—who fueled the fire of hatred.

The constant surveillance of our movements around town by the San Jose Police Department only added to the stress. Some officers, who were friends looking out for me, followed us out of concern. I later learned that one of the individuals involved in our case had falsely reported to both the San Jose Fire Department and the Police Department that I was carrying a firearm. The truth was that I had never carried a weapon; I understood that any misjudgment could be weaponized against me. One day, while meeting my attorney, Allen Ruby, in court, a police officer searched me in front of the co-complainants—a humiliating display that revealed a mole within our group.

Another unsettling moment unfolded when Linda and I attended a play at San Jose State University. Spotting Regina Williams—the San Jose city manager and one of the plaintiffs in the reverse discrimination lawsuit—standing in the lobby, I noticed the fear etched on her face as she approached two police officers. The police officers approached me; I reassured them that I posed no threat and wanted to avoid embarrassment for Linda. Later, I learned that Williams had requested the officers to frisk me before I entered the theater. Fortunately, they deemed it inappropriate, choosing instead to remain close for her comfort.

As we walked into the theater, I could see Regina casting fearful glances back at us, although police officers flanked her. For Linda, attending events at San Jose State was a way of supporting her colleagues, and we were familiar faces among the audience that night. Yet, these tense encounters with law enforcement constantly reminded us of our diminished freedom to move freely throughout our community. The hostile attitudes from neighbors further strained our relationship, compelling us to consider a move to Monterey. This change would not only alleviate our distress but also bring Mr. Turner closer to his family.

MOVING TO MONTEREY

After an extensive search throughout Monterey County, Linda finally found a house in Del Rey Oaks, a small town between Seaside and Monterey. The home featured three bedrooms and two bathrooms, with one bathroom conveniently located near Mr. Turner's room, making it easier to care for him. We initially tried renting in Monterey, Pacific Grove, and Carmel. However, in 1997, these cities were still plagued with racists who were unwilling to rent to Black people. On several occasions, when we showed up to view a house, the realtor either "forgot" the keys or informed us that the property had just been rented. Seaside, on the other hand, had a shortage of houses within our budget that met our need for a two-bathroom house.

Ultimately, we hired a realtor to find us a suitable house. The house in Del Rey Oaks was nearly perfect. To qualify for the rental, we had to demonstrate substantial financial stability, provide our bank statements, and prove our creditworthiness before the owners agreed to rent to us. Upon further investigation of the property, Linda discovered that the original deed included ownership restrictions against Blacks, Jews, and Filipinos, a stark reminder of the area's racist past.

After moving into the house in Del Rey Oaks, we arranged for Mr. Turner to be medevaced from Stanford to our new home. The Monterey oncology services were excellent, and the doctors treated Mr. Turner with great care and respect. He had daily caregivers that helped us manage his comfort level. Linda's mother and sisters visited Mr. Turner often, which brought him a sense of joy. His son Charles Dumas, an actor and full professor at Penn State, who lived in Pennsylvania, visited Mr. Turner twice before his passing. These visits also helped Linda reconnect with her brother, who continued to visit and support her.

One day, while Linda walked on the beach, I was left to care for Mr. Turner. He asked, "Did you ever think you would have to care for me?" I responded, "No, I never thought about it, but I am more than willing to help." Mr. Turner was extremely ill and died within two months in hospice care on November 27, 1997. Linda's mother lived five years after Mr. Turner's death. Despite knowing she was seriously ill, we could not convince her to see a doctor. Finally, she was taken to the Monterey Community Hospital, where Linda introduced her to a doctor. It was determined that she had stomach cancer. Mrs. Turner died peacefully on January 17, 2002, at the home of Linda's youngest sister, Leza, in Marina, California, just two blocks from where we lived.

After Mr. Turner's funeral, I agreed to stay in Monterey. We followed my mother's advice: find a church and become a member. I started playing golf and met a golfer who was a First Baptist Church of Pacific Grove member. The member I admired most was Deacon Bill Story. He liked us, especially Linda because she had a doctorate degree by then. Story and his wife owned a home in Pacific Grove; they were one of a handful of Black people who lived there. He was a lieutenant general, and his wife was a high school teacher. They were highly educated, and held prestigious careers and middle-class wealth. About 10 percent of the congregation was my age or younger. The older members liked us, so I joined the church, taught Sunday school classes, and attended church business meetings.

Deacon Story introduced Linda to Dorothy Lloyd, the dean of the Teacher Education Department at California State University, Monterey Bay (CSUMB), in 1998. This introduction resulted in Linda getting hired to teach diversity and sociology courses for the Liberal Studies Department. Linda ultimately retired from CSUMB after eighteen years of teaching. While Linda nurtured her new career, I played golf thrice weekly with partners Gene Symone, Aaron Shinault, and Don Williams. Of course, I was the weakest golfer at first. But playing with three brothers became the highlight of my week.

THE SECOND FEDERAL TRIAL

At the end of the first federal trial, it was discovered that when the city manager, Regina Williams, left California, she also left behind unreported files, including seventy papers regarding the San Jose Fire Department and the plaintiffs who had filed a reverse discrimination lawsuit. The San Jose city attorney argued that the documents had no substance that could have changed the juror's decision. However, Allen Ruby had other thoughts:

> Allen Ruby argued that some items could have been used to contradict testimony by former City Manager Regina V. K. Williams and others. "For instance, Williams testified she had not pursued a settlement with fire captains who sued after failing a 1995 promotional exam. But the documents included a five-point settlement offer in her writing." Ruby convinced Chief Magistrate Judge Edward Infante that the materials were central to several issues in the civil trial: the discipline imposed on Bynoe, the views of Dorman and Regina Williams about the plaintiffs, and the existence of racism in the department.[1]

I was leery of participating in a second federal trial, but the other plaintiffs were hopeful for a win. After all, Ray Brooks had won his court

---

1. Mowatt, "Retrial Opens."

case, suing the City of San Jose for illegal termination. The first trial ended as a mistrial, but they were encouraged by this new information found in Regina Williams's office. The vote of eight to three received from the jury from our first trial was also in our favor. Ruby wanted to pursue a retrial; he believed in our case and that he could prove that we had been discriminated against. Ruby and Chapman were highly prepared to present this case in a way that limited the San Jose Fire Department and the City of San Jose from presenting unfounded information about any of the plaintiffs. They were diligent in their approach, allowing the plaintiffs to express themselves openly and with emotional determination. The San Jose city attorney also learned new ways to present their case using additional, highly prepared witnesses. Their purpose was to impress the jurors. During the first trial, some of the city's witnesses were ill-equipped intellectually to answer questions. The retrial in the US District Court in San Jose started on May 8, 1999, and lasted four weeks. The limitations imposed on the trial by the judge made it challenging for Ruby to prove racism, specifically by the San Jose city manager and the San Jose Fire Department's Chief Robert Dorman.

I traveled from Monterey to San Jose several days every week to confer with my attorneys throughout the preparation for the second trial. My co-complainants were optimistic about the appeal. Once the second trial started, all plaintiffs were in ready form; the dress code and seating arrangement remained unchanged. Fewer people and supporters attended the second trial. My mother, at age eighty-two, the most important person in my life, took an airplane from New York City to Monterey and stayed until the end of the trial. My mother sat next to Linda, and on our drive back to Monterey, she made many observations of concern. She knew my detractors and could identify their positions in the fight. She was astute about the jury, commenting that they were typical white jurors, marginally educated, working-class, biased, and racist. My mother even noted the number of jurists who fell asleep throughout the court sessions. She was troubled by the court's rules and limitations but kept encouraging me to stay the course.

Several church members attended the trial and were impressed by the dignity of the Black firefighters and the levels of discrimination imposed on them as city employees during the 1990s. Many church members had never observed a trial of this magnitude. They expressed what they learned during Sunday's church services and requested prayer for all the Black firefighters. My position in the church was elevated because of my civil rights engagements. We lost the case overwhelmingly. While sad this time, I knew we would have a new life in Monterey. I started planning ways to become a purposeful citizen, determined to find a place and way to help the Seaside community. I visited Black churches and organizations designed to help children and teenagers in need, a concern I felt passionate about. I continued to play golf and meet some of the community's Black leaders. I requested and received several letters of recommendation from fire chiefs and political leaders throughout the country. These leaders wanted to help me establish a new life in Monterey. But the leaders of Seaside were skeptical; we were outsiders. We had left Seaside for over thirty years.

I will forever be grateful to Allen Ruby for taking my case to the United States Court of Appeals for the Ninth Circuit, even though we ultimately lost for the final time. The official determination was that the trial court denied our claims. Despite this setback, I felt that with the support of excellent attorneys, dedicated coplaintiffs, and two rigorous trials, I had kept my word and fought to the best of my ability to secure a win for the SCCBFA against the systemic racism that was all too evident in the San Jose Fire Department.

THE CASE IS OVER—BACK TO THE FAMILY

Linda worked to improve her teaching career at CSUMB, and I developed relationships with the Black community. I finally started receiving my retirement pay from the San Jose Fire Department in late 1998. It took two years to receive a pension check because the CETA years were never counted. Before receiving my retirement, we lived off our savings and Linda's small salary from the university. In 1999, my granddaughter Ruby Rose graduated from high school and was accepted into the Fashion Institute of Design and Merchandising (FIDM), a two-year private college in San Francisco, California. I helped her find an apartment near Lake Merritt in Oakland, California, and I visited her at least twice a month or whenever she needed me. Ruby supported herself by working at an eyeglass company, LensCrafters, and also received financial help from her mother. After graduating from FIDM, she attended New York University (NYU) in New York City. I found her a studio apartment near the Brooklyn Bridge in Fort Greene. Linda and I visited Ruby and my mother in New York City at least four times a year for three years, offering Ruby emotional and financial support as she navigated NYU and spent time with my aging mother.

Linda and I treasured the moments we shared with my mother, who had lived in the same apartment at 2508 7th Ave, Apartment 3, in the heart of Harlem, New York, for over fifty years. She also owned a candy store and a newspaper stand in Harlem for many years. Every time I visited, I rented a car to take her to Long Island or wherever else she wanted to go throughout the boroughs. Those outings with my mother were the highlight of my time in New York. At eighty-nine, I knew she didn't have much time left, so I tried to convince her to move to California. But she loved New York City too much to leave; her friends were there, and she just couldn't make the transition. My brother even advised me that moving her might not improve her quality of life and could hasten her decline. After a fall on her apartment staircase, my mother moved to upstate New York to live with my sister. She passed away from heart failure on June 17, 2006. My entire family attended her funeral, except for my brother Myles. Losing her was deeply painful for me—I suddenly felt lost in New York, almost like an orphan. It took time for me to appreciate just how lucky I was to have had my mother in my life for so long.

When life began to feel normal again, the fire department no longer held sway over me, and my golf game improved. Our finances were tight, so Linda and I moved into faculty housing at CSUMB. The condo in Marina, north of Monterey, was more affordable and helped us save nearly a thousand dollars monthly. Marina, however, was a small, quiet town—less progressive, foggy, and lacking in activities. Still, the move gave me the time and space to find peace with myself and my accomplishments. I had survived the terror of anti-Black racism deeply ingrained in the San Jose Fire Department, and that resilience had been critical to my ability to keep fighting for justice. I was often reminded that the challenges I faced were minor compared to what my ancestors had endured. My daughter Nicola lived in our house in San Jose, while Traci resided in Fremont, California, with her second husband. I had no worries about the future—opportunities were always there when I chose to seek them out.

A NEW CAREER IDEA

One afternoon in 2001, while watching the evening news, I saw the mayor of Salinas, Anna M. Caballero, the first woman mayor elected in the 126-year history of the City of Salinas. I had previously given a lecture at CSUMB with her about community service and the city and county services available to her constituents. On this particular day, she was on the local news introducing the new police chief, Dan Ortega. I knew Ortega from his time as the deputy chief of the San Jose Police Department. Caballero and Ortega were discussing the alarming gang crimes plaguing the small town of Salinas, California, about fifteen miles from Monterey. They were unveiling a new initiative aimed at middle school students, those still young enough to be steered away from gang involvement. Many of these youth had relatives who were gang members and were at risk of being recruited into gangs either by choice or necessity. They announced a summit to address the issue and sought solutions.

I attended the summit, and when I saw Ortega, we embraced; he remembered me. During the summit, I had the opportunity to share a leadership program and curriculum that Linda had developed for middle school children. Police Chief Ortega and Mayor Anna Caballero supported the program and its curriculum. Within six months, we collaborated with Mayor Caballero, who secured a significant grant for a leadership education program for Latino youth.

In 2002, we were hired to teach leadership classes primarily for middle school children who were mostly Latino, low-income, and some who only spoke Spanish. The program allowed for fifteen students to attend for two weeks during the summer months when children were most vulnerable to gang influences. For two years, we taught two two-week classes each summer, and the program proved to be very successful, garnering heartfelt letters from students over the years.

Two students who frequently emailed us were accepted to CSUMB, and another attended UCLA. The class was so successful that enrollment in the second year included a few white students and two Black students whose parents had political connections to secure their inclusion. It was fascinating to witness different groups learn to accept one another's differences and share knowledge. By the end of the second year's classes, several female students hosted sleepovers at their homes, while others made short visits among themselves. This was just the beginning for many students as they learned to value education and appreciate diverse cultures.

However, by the end of the second year, Linda and I felt we had become too exhausted for the job; our energy was depleted at the end of each day. Although we had hired two students from CSUMB to assist us, it became too much for us to continue. After our daily routine of teaching and interacting with the students, all we could manage was to go home and sleep; those young students honestly wore us out.

Chapter 15

Dad, I Have the Big C

LIFE'S GREATEST TRIALS OFTEN come when least expected, testing the depths of our resilience and the strength of familial bonds. This chapter chronicles a profoundly personal and heartbreaking period in Trusty's life—the battle against cancer that claimed his beloved youngest daughter, Traci. It captures the raw pain of facing a problem he could neither control nor solve, a stark contrast to the challenges Trusty had navigated throughout his career and personal life. Amidst this struggle, the family united to provide Traci with love, comfort, and dignity, challenging a healthcare system often dismissive of Black patients' humanity. This chapter reflects not only the sorrow of losing a child but also the strength found in faith, community, and the indelible memories shared in her final days. It is a deeply emotional journey through grief, resilience, and the unbreakable bond of a father's love.

As I started living retired and enjoying most days golfing and hanging out with my dog and friends, "The Big C" would rear its ugly head again, but this time it was my baby daughter. This chapter is about having to deal with the most difficult problem I have ever had in life. A problem I had no control over or plans to fix. My daughter had cancer.

Shortly after the leadership program ended, I had my first heart surgery in 2004 at the age of sixty. It was December, and Linda became concerned that I was listless after playing golf and usually slept for hours. She insisted that I see a doctor. I saw my general practitioner, Doctor Kennedy, within a few days. He was immediately alarmed, stating that I had a severe heart valve problem. Dr. Kennedy arranged for me to see Dr. Clark, a well-known heart specialist in Monterey. Dr. Clark assessed that my aortic valve was functioning at a 25 percent capacity, a condition that could cause an immediate heart attack. Linda and I had planned a trip to New York to be with my mother for the holidays, but with this diagnosis, Linda insisted that I have the surgery immediately. She canceled the trip and started making plans for my surgery. I tried to postpone the date till after the holidays, but Linda insisted that I have the surgery immediately. She even informed my golf partners that I wasn't playing golf again until after I recovered from the surgery.

The five-hour surgery to replace an aortic valve was done at Stanford Medical Center by one of the top heart surgeons in the country, Dr. Robert Robbins. Linda stayed near the hospital, and Traci arrived every morning to walk with me. Nicky visited a couple of times but called several times throughout the day. I survived the ordeal; I even visited Ruby Rose in Brooklyn, New York, while recovering. Ruby Rose almost killed me by insisting I run with her throughout the city. She wanted to help me strengthen my heart. Traci brought me a dog, a cute little white Maltese who weighed about ten pounds. Sadie became my best friend; while Linda was at work, Sadie kept me entertained and provided a routine. I had to walk her three times daily, which helped me get fit. We continued to live comfortably in CSUMB's faculty housing in Marina, California. The housing was located in the country, a natural habitat for wild animals such as skunks, coyotes, wild turkeys, and boar. The condo house was much larger than the prior home in Del Rey Oaks, with space for us to spread out.

After my surgery, Linda began planning for her retirement and searching for our final home. She wanted a house within walking distance of town and the beach. It took us two years to find a home that would suit us. I must admit that I stalled as long as possible; I wasn't particularly interested in buying another house. However, an excellent real estate agent, Jan Pratt continued to find exciting houses and kept us involved in the search. We had purchased homes several times before, and I found the process stressful. Many of the houses within our budget were just two bedrooms, one bath, and about eight hundred square feet.

When the housing market collapsed in 2008, it significantly affected Monterey, leading to lower prices. During this downturn, we found a 1,380-square-foot, three-bedroom, two-bath cottage near downtown Monterey, just five blocks from the beach. It was a house we could afford, though it needed renovation. With the assistance of two young Mexican brothers who were contractors, I had the kitchen remodeled before Linda moved in.

For about a month, Sadie and I lived in the new house, just the two of us. Traci started coming home more frequently and wanted to be a part of our lives. She even helped us move from faculty housing over a weekend during one of her visits. We continued to make changes to the house, tackling one project each year until we were satisfied with the outcome. Nicky still lived in our San Jose home, while Traci resided in Austin, Texas, with her third husband. The most surprising and significant moment for many Black people, including me, was when Barack Obama won the presidential election in 2008, becoming the first African American president. I was ecstatic and made a point to watch his transition every time he appeared on television.

TRACI AND THE BIG C

Trouble is always lurking in the background. Just as our family was growing closer, I received my first ever text message, and it was from Traci. The message read, "Dad, I have the Big C." As a girl dad, both girls always called me first if they were in trouble. I quickly tuned up my car and drove to Austin, Texas the next day. Linda arrived by plane within a week to be there for the biopsy. The results were devastating. Traci had stage four lung cancer with an estimated twelve months to live. The doctors explained that there was nothing they could do to extend her life.

I stayed with Traci, taking her to chemotherapy sessions and other medical appointments for forty-five days. Despite the grim prognosis, she was determined to beat the illness. The chemo made her incredibly sick, and it broke my heart to see her in so much pain, crying for hours. Linda took a semester off from teaching and moved in with Traci for the next few weeks. We were dissatisfied with the treatment Traci received from the oncology doctors in Austin and Houston, particularly their treatment of Black patients. Many Black cancer patients were subjected to extreme experimental chemotherapy trials, leaving them lifeless and in severe pain, and their skin was blackened significantly.

As we watched Traci's health decline, it became clear that the doctors were more interested in experimenting than in providing her with a quality of life. Linda convinced Traci to move to Monterey, where we hoped she would receive more humane treatment—care that valued her life and aimed to make her as comfortable as possible.

A poignant image of Trusty standing in front of a red truck with his loyal white dog, Sadie. The dog was a gift from Traci, and she helped him get through so much sadness.

When Traci sold her home in Texas and moved to Monterey, her quality of life improved drastically. A compassionate woman oncologist in Monterey prescribed medication to counteract the debilitating effects of the chemotherapy. This allowed Traci to regain a sense of normalcy; she could visit friends, chat on the phone with her Texas and Monterey acquaintances, and participate in everyday activities again. I continued to attend church, though Linda did not; she had never believed in organized religion. Despite this, I always considered her one of the most spiritual people I knew. Linda had grown up Catholic but left the faith due to the horrific scandals involving child endangerment by priests. Additionally, we couldn't ever marry in the Catholic Church because I was raised Presbyterian.

We were fortunate to meet Darrell Wesley, a young, dynamic Methodist preacher, at this pivotal moment. His modern interpretation of the Bible resonated with Linda and many younger people in Monterey. We were so impressed with Reverend Wesley that we asked him to officiate Traci's memorial service. During Traci's final days, her oncologist admitted her to the Carmel Community Hospital for a month to provide more care and comfort. When Traci returned home, she accepted these would be her last days. We devoted all our time to caring for and being by her side. It was remarkable how much family history and memorable times we shared during those final moments.

Traci died at our home in Monterey, surrounded by the family. Linda, despite the immense pain of losing her baby girl, handled it with remarkable strength. Reverend Wesley and Marvin Coffee spent countless hours comforting us after Traci's death, making our acceptance of her loss a bit easier. Reverend Wesley did an outstanding job at the memorial, which was attended by many of Traci's friends and firefighters who came to support the family. We were incredibly grateful to have Reverend Wesley in our lives. He spent many hours with Traci and me, helping me understand and process my grief. This time together also prepared him to deliver a heartfelt and meaningful memorial service.

Reverend Wesley seemed to grasp the depth of our loss, and Linda and I were on the verge of tears most days. For months, Linda could barely sleep, only getting up to check on me and Nicola, who had also stayed with her sister throughout her final days. We found solace in their loving conversations, which helped mend many past misunderstandings. I often felt helpless but was somewhat relieved that Traci was no longer suffering. Still, I couldn't stop myself from tearing up frequently and unexpectedly. Traci lived for fourteen months after her diagnosis and passed away quietly on November 21, 2010, six days before her forty-third birthday. Reverend Wesley has been a member of our small family since 2009. Linda and I found his teachings soulful and exciting; he is a teacher, not just a minister. Reverend Wesley left the Monterey area in 2013 but returns often as a visiting minister for several small churches in Monterey, where he started his civilian career. Whenever he is in Monterey, you can be sure we make a connection. He has, on occasion, introduced me as his surrogate father; we talk at least once a month about anything, regardless of where he is. We have included Reverend Wesley in our trust. He will, if able, present at our memorials.

Chapter 16

The Golden Years

THIS CHAPTER REFLECTS THE joy and camaraderie Trusty found in the years after his mother's passing, through shared interests and enduring friendships. With golf as a central theme, it explores how time spent on the greens became a medium for rekindling connections and creating lasting memories. Whether in Southern California with old friends or hosting gatherings during Monterey's vibrant festivals, these experiences exemplify how life's simple pleasures can foster deep bonds and create new traditions.

Amid the backdrop of music, culture, and community, Trusty focused on ensuring his family's well-being, particularly by bringing Nicola closer after Traci's passing. These moments of fellowship and family offered much-needed solace, a reminder that even amid profound loss, the warmth of connection can be a powerful source of healing. It was now time to explore other countries and cultures.

After my mother passed away, I found little reason to visit New York City. Instead, I took solace in reconnecting with friends and fellow Black firefighters in Southern California. I also picked up golf, playing several times a week, and began to truly enjoy the game. Golf became a common interest among my friends in Southern California, leading me to spend time with Russell Steppe in San Diego and Herschel Clady and Ray Brook in Long Beach. Additionally, I made trips to Atlanta to visit Bobby Dixon. Our reunions were a far cry from the ideological clashes of our younger years;

now, we were simply a group of older men enjoying each other's company, sharing stories, and relishing our rounds of golf together.

Though I was still a novice golfer, my friends were kind enough to tolerate my inexperience. Most of them had single-digit handicaps and had been playing for decades. Our go-to course was the historic black course, Chester Washington Golf Course in Los Angeles, though I also loved playing with Russell at Torrey Pines in San Diego, a course that Tiger Woods made famous.

Southern California offered a welcome change from Monterey. The weather was warmer, and the company of friends made it all the better. Brooks and Clady belonged to several Black golf clubs, and every year, they invited Linda and me to their tournament in Palm Springs. That event became a highlight for us. Palm Springs, with its mature population and vibrant jazz and blues clubs, was the perfect place to relax. While I was out on the greens, Linda enjoyed shopping and socializing with the other wives, making it a rewarding experience for both of us.

When I visited Russell in San Diego, he introduced me to the city's beaches and its lively social scene. I quickly grew fond of San Diego's variety and soon became familiar with navigating its freeways. Russell, a member of Brothers United, San Diego's Black firefighters' association, often hosted gatherings at his house. We'd spend hours in his backyard, drinking and discussing everything from politics to world issues, often diving into deep conversations about race and culture. While Russell was at work, I enjoyed spending time with his wife, Sherman, and their sons, Branden and Ryan. Russell was not only a great father but also one of the most generous and spiritual people I knew. Our conversations, whether in person or over the phone, always left me feeling uplifted. He taught me so much about positivity, patience, and the importance of gratitude for the blessings in our lives. Like me, Russell was a history buff and an avid reader. I often joked that he was my brother from another mother.

FRIENDS AT THE MONTEREY BLUES AND JAZZ FESTIVALS

My Black golf partners in Monterey moved to a Salinas golf club because they were disturbed by the increase in course fees, leaving me as the only Black member of the Pacific Grove Golf Club. I started playing golf with several new friends and acquaintances at the Pacific Grove Municipal Golf

Course; they were primarily white golf members. I typically played several times a week with different groups and was a member of Pacific Grove's Seniors Club, which hosted monthly tournaments. I became close to a golfer who had also lost his daughter to illness. Dan McKay was a short-statured Irish man in his 80s. We played golf together until his death.

One day, I received a call from Jerry Floyd, a friend and firefighter from the San Jose Fire Department. Jerry had served as one of the captains at Station 16 during my early years there. After leaving the fire department, he became the owner of an insurance company that specializes in services for firefighters and police officers, achieving remarkable success in the process. When he built a home in Carmel, he reached out to me, and I found myself visiting Jerry every few months. We would play golf, enjoy lunch, or take walks through downtown Carmel.

Jerry was a well-dressed, affluent white man of average height, articulate and generally pleasant. Our presence together created a scene that often bewildered the residents of Carmel. We cherished each other's company, sharing laughter about our shared history and reflecting on our lives as we moved in and out of various shops and restaurants. Jerry always paid the tab, as I reminded him of his financial success—a fact I never hesitated to tease him about.

With Jerry, I felt at ease; he was consistently supportive and attentive to the challenges I faced, never resorting to racial stereotypes or dehumanizing narratives. Occasionally, we would spend time in my town of Monterey, a community at the end of the bay. On one of his visits, Jerry brought his granddaughter and wife to visit Linda. During that visit, his granddaughter discussed colleges with Linda, while Jerry and I underscored the value of our friendship.

MOVING NICOLA TO MONTEREY

In 2011, after the heartbreaking loss of our daughter Traci, we decided to sell our house in San Jose and purchase a condo for Nicola in New Monterey, just two and a half miles from our home. The house in San Jose was too large for Nicola, and without Traci's help, it became overwhelming for me to manage. Additionally, I wanted Nicola to be closer to us for her well-being and safety. To overcome Nicola's initial hesitancy about moving to Monterey, I enticed her with a newer car and a condo that boasted ocean views. Nicola quickly fell in love with her new home and car, and she eventually acclimated to the weather and the compactness of the community. She found a job at the Naval Postgraduate School and continued to visit her friends in San Jose.

MONTEREY FESTIVALS

Although there were plenty of tourist attractions in Monterey, I especially enjoyed the annual Monterey Blues Festival, held every June. Linda and I bought tickets every year until the festival sadly went bankrupt in 2012. One year, I ran into Floyd Hoffman and his wife, Marsha, at the festival. Floyd, who had retired as an assistant chief for the Los Angeles City Fire Department, was known for his financial support of the Los Angeles Stentorians. He also attended regional Black firefighters' meetings, though he rarely spoke up or contributed to the conversation. Floyd liked to refer to himself as "the spook who sat by the door," referencing Sam Greenlee's 1969 novel, *The Spook Who Sat by the Door*. The book tells the fictional story of the first Black CIA officer and explores themes of political subversion, guerrilla warfare, and the systemic racism faced by African Americans in the United States.[1]

The Hoffmans always parked their RV in the Blues Festival parking lot, turning it into a party place for friends and families to gather, socialize, and enjoy themselves. Over time, I started visiting the Hoffmans at their home in Harbor City, a quaint suburban area near Los Angeles. Floyd, who had worked closely with Herschel Clady for many years, was an easygoing individual, as tall and dark-complexioned as I am. Occasionally, his neighbors would mistake me for him.

The second musical venue we favored was the Monterey Jazz Festival. One year, around 2012, I saw Bill Parker at the Jazz Festival; I invited him to my house. Bill was a young Black firefighter who had served as the president of the Los Angeles City Stentorians. Our paths had crossed while I was still working for the San Jose Fire Department. Bill brought along a few of his LA firefighter friends. Although not all of them were members of the Stentorians, they were avid jazz enthusiasts and golfers. We enjoyed the visits and invited Bill and his friends to come back anytime they attended the annual September Monterey Jazz Festival.

We began hosting backyard lunches for Bill Parker and other Black firefighters, along with friends of firefighters who were attending the

1. Greenlee, *Spook*.

Monterey Jazz Festival. The attendees, mostly bachelors, often brought their girlfriends and generously contributed to the luncheon with food and drinks. I would play golf with them on the first and last days of the festival. Our basic lunch spread included drinks, Linda's homemade spaghetti, my barbecued burgers and sausages, and always a dessert. The conversations ranged from Black firefighters to politics, culture, history, and sometimes the newest trivia, but the discussions were always engaging. I believe our guests felt relaxed and welcomed at our home, as they sometimes stayed so long that we missed the early Saturday evening shows. The LA visitors who most often hung out in our backyard included Monte Buchner, Robert Hill, Don Conkrite, Joe Johnson, Winston Roberts, Tracey Hutson, Jennifer Johnson, and Addison Birdine.

We enjoyed our visits with friends in Southern California, but eventually Linda, who loved to travel, became restless and desperately wanted to travel abroad while we were still healthy. During our thirties and forties, we had taken several cruises throughout the Caribbean and South America. While Linda grew up and traveled with her family as a military dependent to Japan and Europe, she later traveled on her own, to Indonesia and Cuba.

Chapter 17

World Travelers

IN THIS CHAPTER, TRUSTY takes you on his first international journey to Italy, a dream long in the making that came to life in November 2014. The experience was not just about seeing Venice, Florence, and Rome; it was about bonding with fellow travelers and immersing ourselves in the rich tapestry of Italian culture. Trusty vividly remembers gliding through the canals of Venice, the thrill of living out a moment he had long imagined. However, amidst the beauty, Trusty grappled with the deep sorrow of missing a friend's funeral back home.

The chapter captures the duality of joy and pain, as well as the strength found in the support of loved ones during his medical trials. Trusty's heart was full as he returned home, unaware of the challenges that lay ahead—a second surgery that would test his resolve and resilience. Trusty recounts his emotional return to travel after surgery, this time to South Africa in August 2015. The trip was a transformative experience, allowing him to connect with the profound history of the land and its people. As Trusty explored the townships and engaged with residents, he felt a stirring recognition of shared struggles. The protests he witnessed in Soweto reminded him of the ongoing fight for justice, echoing his own battles back home. This chapter beautifully intertwines the beauty of African landscapes with the painful legacy of apartheid, revealing the resilience that fuels our collective quest for dignity. The journey not only reignited Trusty's spirit but also deepened his understanding of identity and purpose, culminating in a powerful sense of gratitude for life's lessons.

HAIL ITALY—2014

Our first international trip was a bus tour of Italy in November 2014. I felt invigorated and excited to immerse myself in the rich history and culture of the sites we explored. The tour included three Black couples, one Black family and fifteen other travelers, all eager to experience the beauty of Venice, Florence, Rome, and the Amalfi Coast. It was thrilling to finally see these iconic places in person, fulfilling my long-held dream of gliding through Venice's canals by gondola while singing "O Sole Mio." I even assisted other travelers in getting on and off as they navigated the gondola.

In Rome, the city was alive with tourists, and we expertly navigated through crowds gathered around historic landmarks. The Colosseum was breathtaking, its ancient structure a testament to history. Our insightful travel guide shared captivating stories about its role in ancient entertainment. Each location left a lasting impression, complemented by the unforgettable cuisine and wines. We formed a close bond with Marion and Ramona Orr, a remarkable Black couple from Providence, Rhode Island. Marion, a full professor at Brown University, and Ramona, a senior policy analyst, were memorable companions. However, I regretted missing Floyd Hoffman's funeral while enjoying Italy.

When we returned home, I still felt energized, unaware of the medical challenges ahead. Soon after, my cardiologist informed me that I needed a second aortic valve replacement, this time with a cow valve. The news was jarring, recalling the agony of my first surgery. However, I went ahead with the procedure, which lasted nine hours due to additional complications.

During my recovery at Stanford Hospital, my firefighter friends, including Lacy Atkinson and Ola, supported Linda throughout my time in intensive care. Linda and Nicola were the first comforting visitors I had when I emerged from intensive care. While Nicola was understandably worried, it was Linda who offered me the strength to endure the pain. Additionally, my godfamily, led by my closest friend, Carl, visited and encouraged me despite their private struggles. Their presence during this challenging time was a source of great strength when I needed it most. Six months later, I was ready to travel again. It was almost as if I felt the urgency to see the world before my inevitable death.

SOUTH AFRICA—2015

Six months following my surgery, my longing to travel was reignited, though I would feel weakened after the grueling sixteen-hour flight to Johannesburg. Beyond the simple desire to explore new places, I sensed an urgent need to experience as much of the world as possible. Linda and I planned the trip to South Africa, a destination I had long dreamed of visiting. I wanted to see the beautiful landscapes of Cape Town and the rich history of Johannesburg, and the profound experience of standing on Robben Island—where Nelson Mandela had been imprisoned—exceeded my expectations. This journey was not merely a vacation; it stirred something deep within me.

I eagerly anticipated this next adventure, understanding that travel had transformed from a simple pursuit of new sights into a vital opportunity for growth and evolution, regardless of my age or the challenges that lay ahead. In August 2015, Linda and I embarked on the deeply emotional journey to South Africa, Durban, and Zimbabwe. In South Africa, I was warmly welcomed as I explored the Black townships, engaging in conversations with residents and sampling traditional foods despite our tour guide's advice against eating at the township markets. We met Fred and Penny Horton, a Black couple, on our bus tour, and we quickly formed a bond. After a few days, the four of us hired a local Black taxi driver to take us to the famous township of Soweto.

When we arrived in Soweto, I felt both disappointed and a bit apprehensive. The township's youth were in the midst of a protest against the government, angered by a ten-day lack of electricity and clean water. Fires burned in the streets, water pails were thrown at official vehicles, and young people sang and shouted as they surged through the streets. Sensing the danger, we quickly left the protest area. Our driver explained the complex social dynamics of South Africa, particularly the divisions among Africans based on skin color and language. He shared that three-quarters of South Africa's population were Black Africans, including Zulu, Xhosa, Sotho, and Tswana people, while the remaining population consisted of Indians, Europeans, and mixed-race individuals. The racial hierarchy typically categorizes people as Black, white, colored, or Indian.

As we toured the townships and absorbed South Africa's painful yet inspiring history, I found myself reflecting on my struggles back home—battles with the fire department, racism, and the ongoing fight for justice. The resilience of the Black South African people reminded me that the quest for freedom and dignity is a universal one. Their enduring spirit re-ignited my sense of purpose and resolve. Although I was still on the path to physical recovery, my spirit felt rejuvenated. Each new place we explored added richness to my life as if the world itself were imparting lessons in perseverance, endurance, and the importance of standing tall in the face of adversity. I would return home with a profound sense of gratitude for the chance to move forward, even when the odds seemed insurmountable.

The tour of Robben Island in Cape Town provided a profound histori-cal insight into the imprisonment of Nelson Mandela, who endured twen-ty-seven years of confinement as a result of his resistance to the apartheid regime. This experience stirred complex emotions within me, combining feelings of sadness and anger. While the conditions of the cell itself did not come as a surprise, I felt deep frustration towards the oppressive apart-heid government for subjecting prominent Black leaders to such appalling circumstances. Conversely, I also felt immense pride in Mandela's remark-able fortitude, resilience, and ability to maintain both mental and physical strength throughout his incarceration.

Our itinerary included a visit to the Mandela Museum, located in his former residence, where we honored his legacy. The museum featured an array of memorabilia from Mandela's early life, including significant tools and artifacts like books and communication devices that held personal sig-nificance for him. Although the home was sparsely furnished, the visible bullet holes served as a stark testament to the violent history he endured, reminding us of the ongoing struggle for freedom and justice.

On the occasion of our final dinner at the hotel in South Africa, I wore a dashiki emblazoned with Mandela's image. This gesture was met with a respectful salute from a line of South African men, many of whom identified as Zulu. Their acknowledgment seemed to reflect an appreciation for my embodiment of solidarity as a tall, dark Black man from the United States, honoring their nation and its revered leader.

Our explorations in Durban and Zimbabwe unveiled a remarkable diversity of landscapes and showcased the inherent beauty of the African people, who moved with grace throughout the countryside. I observed in-dividuals engaging in various activities, from transporting baskets on their heads to laboring in sugar fields or enjoying leisure time by the roadside while awaiting public transportation. The striking beauty of their rich Black skin and robust physiques inspired a profound sense of connection and a deeper understanding of authenticity in our shared heritage.

Both Zimbabwe and Durban operate within the framework of multi-party parliamentary democracies, marked by a constitutional commitment to majority rule and a presidential term limit of five years. Our accommodations in luxurious hotels provided spacious comfort and seamlessly integrated wildlife roaming in their natural surroundings. Among the recreational areas, monkeys and other small animals roamed freely, adding to the unique charm of the environment. From our hotel room in Durban, we were fortunate to catch a glimpse of elephants in the distance, assembling at a natural lake—a sight that left an indelible mark on my memory. These visions only enriched the river safaris, where we saw hippopotamuses, buffalos, crocodiles, and other large and small water animals. We also toured a land safari, where we encountered giant elephants that entertained us, Cape buffalo, giraffes, rhinoceroses, zebras, kudu (my favorite), and more. We never saw the big cats; all of our safari trips occurred too early in the morning to see the cats in their natural habitat.

The bonds we forged during this journey with our friends the Hortons have continued to thrive beyond our travels. We have maintained our connection through visits to each other's homes and vacations in Palm Springs in 2020. This trip stands out as one of the most memorable experiences of my life, highlighting the importance of cultural exchange and the lasting impact of shared history.

When I returned to the United States, I rented a car and visited my childhood best friend, Johnny Dorsett, in Baltimore. When I arrived at his apartment, I found him waiting for me in the parking lot, seated in a wheelchair. As soon as he spotted me, he sprang out of the chair, enveloped me in a hug, and spun me around. I was equally thrilled to see him after at least forty years apart. Our time together was truly special as we reminisced and caught up on each other's lives. At the time, Johnny was bravely fighting cancer, which made our reunion all the more significant. Although he had never met my daughters, he gifted me an old gold watch for Nicola, which she treasures to this day. Tragically, Johnny passed away shortly after our visit, but the timing of our reunion was truly fortuitous.

Upon my return home from South Africa, I learned that one of my very good friends, Benny Clark from the Las Vegas Clark County Black Firefighters Association, had died. It became apparent that I had reached that age when losing close friends happened too often. I called Vergus Porter, another member of the Black Firefighters of Las Vegas, to discuss ways to make it easy for the old-timers to connect with their peers and their associations. We believed that there should be an annual reunion where retired firefighters could not only have fun and meet with their peers but could also be the living history for younger Black firefighters and their organizations. We called Dave Washington, retired fire chief of the Las Vegas Fire Department, and asked him to help us set up the reunion in Las Vegas. We called it a reunion because we had been a family as we fought for jobs and our rights. Vergus, Dave, and I agreed that there would be no scheduled business discussions or political debates. We wanted discussions to be natural and spontaneous, prompting generational reciprocity. It took about a year to work through the logistics for the reunion and to locate all the retired firefighters. We had our first Retired Firefighters Reunion in November 2016.

Italy—Trusty and Linda.

Chapter 18

Connecting with Relatives and Lifelong Friends

CHAPTER 18 IS A rich tapestry of family, friendship, and international travels that shaped Trusty's outlook on life. In 2016, the family ventured to Barbados to celebrate his daughter Nicola's fiftieth birthday, spending time in the warmth of family connections with cousins Albert and Orville Agard. The trip was a joyful reunion, filled with laughter, delicious Bajan cuisine, and the serene beauty of the island's beaches. Dudley had the opportunity to hang out with his godson Myles for his wedding to Gabby in Las Vegas. It was a joy to see them so happy.

Shortly after, the first Retired Black Firefighters Reunion brought together old friends and colleagues, reinforcing the bonds formed through shared dedication and service, and ended with four Black Firefighters Reunions before the pandemic, This chapter also reflects on Trusty's international travels and cross-country visits to close friends and family. Each travel experience enriched his life, broadening his perspectives and deepening his appreciation for the diverse tapestry of culture. These experiences illuminate the importance of community, the power of shared history, and the joy of reconnecting with loved ones across the globe.

FAMILY VACATION WITH BAJAN FAMILY—2016

In 2016, Linda, Nicola, my cousin Vine from New Haven, Connecticut, and I visited our cousins in Barbados, Albert and Orville Agard. Linda and I had visited Barbados thirty-five years earlier, so it was a pleasant trip to see my cousins and their families again. We stayed at an all-inclusive resort area to make it easy for everyone. It was very relaxing: swimming in the warm ocean, hanging out with my cousins, and eating and drinking local food anytime throughout the day. I spent hours showing Nicola around the small island over our seven-day visit. It was a great way to celebrate Nicola's fiftieth birthday. My cousin Albert and his wife, Diane, prepared a birthday dinner for Nicola. They served a Bajan dinner consisting of plantains, rice, chicken, lemon cake, and ice cream and gave Nicola gifts representing Barbados. Our trip home was filled with discussions of family memories.

Every year, we host a block party at our home in Monterey. All the neighbors on our street are invited, and everyone comes. We usually share information about our travels with our neighbors. This particular year, Nicola was the star of the block party. She shared information and pictures about our family in Barbados.

THE FIRST RETIRED BLACK FIREFIGHTERS REUNION—2016

The Las Vegas Retired Black Firefighters Reunion was held at the Texas Hotel and Casino in Las Vegas, Nevada, in November 2016. The first reunion was a great success; everyone agreed that it was an extremely valuable time since most of the retired firefighters of all ranks were aging, and many had life-threatening ailments. Everyone agreed that a reunion would be held each year and hosted by different firefighter organizations. Many of the fire chiefs and firefighters from around the country attended, played golf, and partied together. Most everyone stayed at the Texas Hotel and Casino in Las Vegas. Many of the firefighters played golf and attended the hotel's nightclub party to drink, dance, talk shit, and enjoy each other. Most of the wives appreciated the hotel amenities and shopping in Las Vegas, while a few of the wives played golf. There was something for everyone to do and enjoy. Before dinner, we met in the Meet and Greet Hall to have free hors d'oeuvres and drinks (mostly alcohol) set up and paid for by the three hosting firefighters: Dave Washington, myself, and Vergus Porter. The

Retired Firefighters Reunion represented the Southwest Region, including Arizona, California, Colorado, Hawaii, Nevada, New Mexico, and Utah. A few of the organizations did not have representatives. Most attendees were from California, Arizona, Nevada, and New Mexico. California was well represented: Ollie Linson, Bill Parker, Harry Jackson, Roland Hooks, Teresa De Loch Reed, Ray Brooks, Herschel Clady, Marvin Coffee, Russell Steppe, Mike Smith, Lonnie McDowell, and Al Nero.

VISITS WITH FAMILY AND FRIENDS—2017

The purpose of our travels in 2017 was to visit friends and family through-out the United States. When we arrived in New York, I rented a car. First, Linda, Nicola, and I went to my mother's apartment where Terry, my brother, now lived. Our encounter was admirable since we had not seen each other since my mother's death. Then we visited family and friends on Long Island: Daphne, Leila, Diane, my cousins, and a childhood friend, Bobby White. Later, we went to Connecticut to see my cousin Vine. The family was as I remembered them; as with many families, interactions and communications were complicated. After spending several days with my relatives, we drove to Wilmington, Delaware, to visit the friends we met in South Africa, Penny and Fred Horton. Wilmington was near Philadelphia, so we had the opportunity to spend the day with Linda's brother, Charles Dumas, and his wife, Jo. Linda's brother and wife took us on a tour of the Independence National Historical Park in Philadelphia. Nicola enjoyed the life-size statues, and I liked reading about the laws of the time. Linda enjoyed the time hanging out with her brother. The last part of the trip was our participation at Linda's family reunion in Richmond, Virginia. Linda's cousin, Sharon Todd Williamson, was a gracious host for the event and helped Nicola and me learn a lot about Linda's family, even her younger second and third cousins that we had never met. Sharon stood out as a genuine person with no pretense or malice. The family took a tour of Richmond and found the Black History Museum and Cultural Center of Richmond; it had many interesting stories about Black entrepreneurs and their part in building Richmond. Nicola enjoyed shopping for memorabilia, while Linda enjoyed meeting younger family members and learning more about the history of Richmond.

When we returned home, Linda gifted me a new puppy to replace Sadie, who lived for eleven years but died from cancer in 2016. My newest companion was a ten-week-old Shih Tzu who weighed about five pounds. I had just finished reading Assata Olugbala Shakur's autobiography, so of course, I named my new companion Assata. She was not as protective as Sadie but just as lovable and attentive. We went everywhere together and walked around our Monterey neighborhood thrice daily.

RETIRED BLACK FIREFIGHTERS REUNION—2017

Shortly after we returned home, the second Retired Black Firefighters Reunion was hosted by Russell Steppe and his wife, Shemane. It was supported by the Brothers United, San Diego's Black firefighters' association; this event was a stark contrast to the glitzy Las Vegas gathering. It had a more intimate, family-oriented vibe that made everyone feel right at home. The first event was a picnic on the beach, where seasonal barbecue mingled with the scent of the ocean. There were vegetarian dishes, several meat options, dessert selections, and a variety of drinks to cater to every palate. It was a great relaxing opportunity for everyone to freely recognize each other and enjoy pleasant conversations.

The meet and greet space was strategically located in the heart of the hotel, making it a breeze for everyone to come together and share stories. The hotel's thoughtful accommodations ensured that sharing cars and exploring the vibrant city of San Diego was effortless. For the grand finale of the reunion, Kelly Osby, the wife of Chief Robert Osby, rented a lively Mexican restaurant in the middle of Old Town. She invited everyone from the reunion to a special eightieth birthday bash for Chief Robert Osby. The restaurant was full of excitement as it comfortably hosted all the attendees, along with Chief Osby's family and friends. The atmosphere was full of laughter and conversations filling the air as everyone indulged in a feast fit for the chief. The highlight of the evening was the heartfelt and often hilarious roasts of Chief Osby. Firefighters took turns sharing their funniest and most profound stories of working with the chief, each tale adding to the tapestry of his successful career.

As the night wore on, the party moved back to the meet and greet room, where the camaraderie continued. Drinks flowed, and conversations grew more animated as old friends reconnected and new friendships excelled. The room was alive with the sound of laughter and the clinking of glasses until the late hours. The San Diego reunion was nothing short of spectacular. It offered everyone a chance to unwind and soak up the

Southern California weather. The beautiful beaches provided a perfect backdrop for relaxation and reconnection. Many of the firefighters who had attended the Las Vegas event were also present, adding a sense of continuity and deepening the bonds of friendship. It was a memorable event that left everyone looking forward to the next reunion.

NEW YORK—2018

In 2018, we were invited to Tuscany, Italy, to visit our Monterey neighbors, Richard and Kelly Keir, at their summer villa. As with our other trips, we first stopped for a three-day stay over in New York City before traveling abroad. I had always wanted to ride a horse-drawn buggy through Central Park. On our second day in New York City, Linda and I rented a horse and buggy driven by a man in a top hat. The day coincided with National Puerto Rican Day, featuring a parade and celebrations in Central Park. It was amazing to see people of every color celebrating together, sharing blankets and sitting areas throughout the park. The music varied from one area to another but somehow harmonized beautifully. After our ride through Central Park, we visited the Schomburg Center for Research in Black Culture in Harlem. We make it a point to stop by the Schomburg Center every time we visit New York City, and this time, it had been renovated and was more impressive than ever. Hanging out for hours in Times Square was also a new adventure for us. After resting, we spent several hours late into the night in Times Square, making sure to have a slice of New York pizza and several martinis. Normally, our visits to New York City were allocated to my mother's wants and needs, but this trip was different. I kept thinking maybe we could rent an apartment and live in New York for a while.

ONWARD TO PARIS!—2019

From New York, we took a flight to Paris, France, changing planes at Heathrow Airport. When we arrived at the Paris Charles de Gaulle Airport, we took a taxi to our hotel and checked into the Madeleine Haussmann. Linda had visited France as a child and always wanted to return. I found France exciting and very chic. I loved people-watching as Linda toured the museums and art galleries. This trip was so romantic; I think it was because we were not on a tour or any particular schedule. We managed to create our tours, making sure to see all the famous places of interest to us: the Louvre

Museum, Versailles Palace, the Eiffel Tower, the Moulin Rouge Dinner Show, and we even took a short Seine River cruise. Some days, we slept in late, enjoying the luxury of not having to catch a tour bus. Our hotel was close to the city center, near the Saint-Eustache Church. We used all available Parisian transportation: buses, trains, subways, and even took a short trip on a moped. Of course, we walked a lot. Contrary to popular belief, we didn't find the people snotty; they were generally very gracious in helping us find our way. It rained most mornings, but the afternoon and evening weather was perfect for us.

Our favorite evening dining experiences were at small city restaurants that showcased live musicians. One of the restaurants, which did not have live singers or musicians, was playing background music from the album *Take Me to the Alley* by Gregory Porter, one of my favorite CDs. It was the first time in many years that I felt like singing. I sang a few lines from the song, "More Than a Woman." A few people in the restaurant clapped and smiled at me. Linda was very surprised and pleased.

From Paris, we flew to my favorite city, Florence, Italy. The rivers, bridges, and giant sculptures in the city squares were a reminder of sixteenth-century Florence. Our hotel, Berchielli, was on the river, overlooking two bridges, the Ponte Vecchio and the Ponte Santa Trinita. We only stayed two nights because we were scheduled to meet Richard Keir at the train station. Richard was our Monterey neighbor who lived in Monterey for half the year and the other half in his villa in Italy. When we arrived at the train station, Richard was waiting for us. We traveled by train to Tuscany's southern Siena Province. Richard picked up his car from a parking station and drove us to the town where his villa was located, Celle sul Rigo. Richard had arranged our stay for a week at the Hotel Sette Querce in the village of San Casciano dei Bagni. We were pleasantly surprised at how beautiful the hotel was. We had a suite that included a kitchen, a living area, a very nice feather bed, and, of course, the traditional large bathroom with a bidet. Our stay in San Casciano dei Bagni was also romantic. We ate well and, with Richard and Kelly as travel guides, we learned so much about Tuscany villages and their histories. It was restful yet exciting. Richard spoke fluent Italian, so he was able to help us with purchases for our friends and neighbors in Monterey.

Our path home included a train from Siena Province to Rome and then a short and comfortable flight to Morocco, the northwest corner of Africa. Upon arrival in Morocco, we encountered a surprising situation. The airport was guarded by gun-toting uniformed police. I was ushered to first class while Linda was shuttled to the economy area under strict police supervision. We never figured out why we were separated, but we understood that we were in a potentially dangerous part of the world, so we complied with the instructions. Once on the Royal Air Morocco airplane, I found Linda at the rear of the plane. She was okay, and her seat was comfortable, so we remained in our assigned seats. I had the luxury of a seat that turned into a cozy bed and all the food and drinks I wanted. I hated the food, so I just had several drinks. After fifteen hours on the plane, we arrived at Washington Dulles International Airport. Of course, we couldn't just go home; we rented a car and drove to a hotel in Washington, DC. The next day, we met Linda's cousin from Richmond, Sylvia Craighead, and toured the National Museum of African American History. We were overwhelmed by the magnitude of information held in the extremely large, newly designed museum. After hours of touring the museum, we met Fred and Penny Horton, the friends we met in South Africa, for dinner in the city. It was another fabulous trip, and it was a great way to end it with friends and family.

RETIRED BLACK FIREFIGHTERS REUNION—2018

When we returned to Monterey, I alone drove to Long Beach to attend the 2018 Retired Black Firefighters Reunion hosted by Herschel Clady and his daughter, Chandra Clady. On the second day of the reunion, Vergus Porter and Dave Washington declared it was my turn to host the next Retired Black Firefighters Reunion in Monterey. Linda was not in Long Beach with me, as she was presenting a proposal for her book at the National Women's Studies Annual Conference in San Francisco. So, I hung out with the golfers and my retired friends. The usual firefighters attended, and although I was tired, it was great to see everyone again and to be seen.

MYLES'S WEDDING

There were so many important events that happened in 2019. In April, Linda, Nicola, and I attended the wedding of my godson, Myles Lacey, to Abigail Martinez-Salas in Las Vegas. Later that month, I attended their second wedding held for Gabby's family in Mexico City, Mexico. It was my first time in Mexico City, and I found it to be like many large cities—overcrowded and crime-infested, with many impoverished people living in the streets. However, the wedding was held in an ancient chapel in the countryside, which was beautiful. Myles was happy, having found a wonderfully talented and intelligent woman who would help him live his best life.

RETIRED FIREFIGHTERS REUNION—2019

The most important event of this year was the Retired Firefighters Reunion, which Linda and I would host in Monterey. Once I accepted the gravity of planning such a large event, I reached out to two people I admired for their organizational skills and leadership: Fire Chief Teresa Deloach Reed and Fire Chief Mike Smith. Linda would also help me with the logistics and follow-through. I started working on the plans at the beginning of 2019.

I selected the Beach Hotel to accommodate lodging for the group. It had rooms overlooking the beautiful Monterey Bay, and working with a young Black manager, I was able to secure reasonable room rates. Teresa was in charge of establishing two golf tournaments and collecting the funds. Mike was responsible for organizing and collecting the funds for the celebratory dinner. The dinner, while expensive, was excellent. I ate very little because I wanted to talk with the guests to ensure everyone was happy. I was pleasantly surprised that several firefighters from Los Angeles came, only for the dinner because they had another engagement the first two days.

I made numerous calls to individuals I wanted to be sure would attend the event. I must have called my friends twenty times to ensure they registered for their hotel rooms before they were sold out and that they would attend the entire weekend of events. I called Vergus on April 2 to talk about the reunion and to encourage him to reserve a hotel room at the Beach Hotel in Monterey as soon as possible. Vergus was in the hospital but claimed he wasn't seriously ill. So, I agreed to call him the next day to check on his health and continue our discussion. When I called the next afternoon, April 3, his wife, Maderia, answered his phone and told me that Vergus had died that morning. I was shocked. Losing Vergus made the need for the reunion more important to me. The shock caused me to falter for a few weeks; I had to pause and rethink my own life. My team—Linda, Teresa, and Mike—helped me regroup and push forward, wanting to have the best possible reunion in honor of Vergus.

I also set up the meet and greet location. I chose the Retired Men's Club in Seaside, California. I had to assure the manager of the club that the proceeds from drink sales would exceed three hundred dollars. The final tally for drinks that evening was more than five hundred dollars. I asked one of my friends, a local caterer, to design the space and menu and prepare and serve the food for our meet and greet on the first night. She prepared so much good food that there was plenty left for the next day. And the decorations were all related to Black firefighters.

On the second day, most of the men and a few women played golf for two days. Teresa negotiated with two golf courses for about thirty players. She was able to keep the price down to less than one hundred dollars for two games per person, a price unheard of in Monterey. Linda rented a van and took the wives on a shopping tour of Monterey, Pacific Grove, and Carmel. After golf and shopping, about fifty people ended up at my house, mostly hanging out in the backyard. I was given one thousand dollars from the Santa Clara County Black Firefighters Association for the food and drinks. The money paid for the meet and greet buffet and the drinks and food after golf and the shopping tour. Everyone seemed to enjoy the camaraderie they experienced throughout the three days. I didn't know my house and yard could hold so many people. Many of the same people who attended the other reunions attended the Monterey reunion, except for Ray Brooks. There were a few new firefighters, officers, friends, and family who had not attended any of the prior reunions, like Deputy Chief Lacy Atkinson, Chief Osby's son Chief Darrell Osby, Gerald Simon, my extended family Carl and his wife, Sabina, and Bridget from Sacramento, and Gail and Darian from Monterey and various other close friends.

On the last day after golf, everyone came to my home for drinks and lunch, and then they left to dress for the dinner that would be held at Domenico's, one of the most respected restaurants on the Monterey wharf overlooking the beach and the bay. Marvin Coffee made an announcement at breakfast the final morning of the reunion to honor me. He said, "Trust took everyone to the 'hood,' then he took us 'home,' and lastly, he took everyone to 'elegance' on the beach. He did this in one weekend." I believe everyone enjoyed the reunion. I was pleased with the outcome but extremely tired. I greatly appreciated my team of organizers: Chief Teresa Deloach Reed, Chief Mike Smith, and Dr. Linda Turner Bynoe. The reunion could not have been as successful without the team. The next reunion was scheduled to occur in Hawaii and was to be hosted by Chief Gerald Simon. (This event was canceled due to the Covid-19 pandemic.)

OUR ANNUAL NEIGHBORHOOD CHRISTMAS PARTY

The 2019 annual Christmas party held at our house included many of our 5th Street neighbors. Everyone seemed to have a good time; of course, I was the bartender until I had too much to drink. Several of our neighbors talked about the fancy cars that were parked on our street during the Black Firefighters Reunion. Reunion guests noticed that our neighbors were out in the street admiring their cars up close. Many of the elite cars were owned by chief officers.

LINDA'S BIRTHDAY WITH FRIENDS

Our next trip was to celebrate Linda's birthday in late February 2020. Our friends from Wilmington, Delaware, Penny and Fred Horton, met us in Palm Springs, where we shared an Airbnb for seven days. Russell and Shemane drove from San Diego to join us for Linda's birthday, and we all had a wonderful time. I think Linda felt truly special; it was her first birthday celebration as an adult. The Airbnb was a charming mid-century modern home with a pool, hot tub, and breathtaking views of the San Jacinto Mountains. We spent our days exploring local attractions, like the Palm Springs Aerial Tramway and the Living Desert Zoo and Gardens. Evenings were filled with laughter, great food, and reminiscing about old times.

When we got home on March 1, 2020, the world had changed—Covid-19 was declared a global pandemic, and suddenly, everyone was gripped by fear of this deadly virus. Given my health risks, I took the isolation seriously. We were fortunate when vaccines were developed and golf courses reopened. Throughout the pandemic, Linda and I played golf every Tuesday and Thursday at six thirty in the morning and sometimes on weekends, too. She may have won every twentieth game, but we both improved our skills, stayed active, enjoyed the fresh air, and, most importantly, stayed safe together. Those two years didn't hold any major events, but life felt good. Nicola wasn't working, so she spent nearly every day with us. Despite the pandemic—a situation that hadn't occurred for over a century, we found a sense of peace in our routine.

BACK ON THE ROAD—VISITING FAMILY

By 2022, after getting every vaccine recommended by the FDA, we started branching out again and socializing with a few people. That summer, my cousin Paulette invited me, Linda, and Nicola to a family reunion on July 4 in Seattle, hosted by her daughter Elanya and her husband, Theo Langford. The drive was refreshing; we stopped for a good night's rest at the Gold Rush Hotel in Oregon and another hotel on the beach during our return. Our Airbnb in downtown Seattle was modern and fully equipped, making us feel right at home. Many of my cousins from the Samuel side of the family were there, including Paul, Vine, Steven and his wife, Barbara, and Paulette, along with their children and grandchildren. This side of the family was also conservative but less intense and closed-minded than my brothers and sister. It was a joy to reconnect with my younger male cousins—they were interesting, accomplished, and fun. After returning home, I reflected on the trip with warmth and good intentions, promising myself that I would get to know my cousins better.

A vibrant group shot of chiefs, firefighters, and Trusty, at
Chief Osby's birthday celebration.

Obituary

Dudley Clifford Bynoe (Trusty)
December 25, 2022

DUDLEY CLIFFORD BYNOE (TRUSTY) was born on July 12, 1944, the third child of the union between Dudley Samuel Bynoe and Ruby Archer Bynoe; he was initially raised in New York City until the time came for him to relocate to Port Jefferson Station, New York, where he lived under the direction of his beloved grandmother Bertha Downes Archer (Granny) and Clifford C. Archer (Grampa).

Dudley believed it was the strong leadership of black women in his life, his mother and grandmother, that helped him to cultivate the strong side of the man we all knew and loved. He always spoke glowingly of his relationship with his mom and Granny. Later in life, he'd build upon that positive feminine foundation as a husband, a "girl dad," and a mentor to female firefighters.

Dudley's nickname, "Trusty," he received as a youngster when he was elected as a "trustee" in a club he had joined in his school years in Port Jefferson. As he grew to be the tall, strong, multitalented man we all knew, he always looked out for those around him, confirming the fact that Trusty was trustworthy.

Trusty was the kind of man who would stand up in situations when others wouldn't; he'd speak with conviction for those who couldn't. He was a powerful man of courage, love, and compassion who would break himself to help family and friends.

In 1962, he was drafted into the US Army, which brought him to the Monterey Peninsula, where he would meet the love of his life, his soulmate, Ms. Linda Turner. Dudley stated that "Linda was beautiful, strong, intelligent, and the perfect match for his heart," so on July 4, 1965, they were married and remained together for fifty-eight years.

Trusty and Linda's love story birthed two beautiful daughters. The firstborn was Nicola (Nicky), and shortly after came their baby girl, Traci. Trusty was protective and loving of his daughters, which earned him the special title of "girl dad."

After leaving the Army, Trusty worked for a time at the Ford Motor Company in Milpitas, California, before joining the San Jose Fire Dept. where he worked for twenty-five years. He spent many of those twenty-five years at Station 16 in the community, near and dear to his heart.

Trusty was the second black man hired by the San Jose Fire Department as a firefighter and was instrumental in helping to add men and women of color to the ranks, thereby diversifying the department.

Trusty was a founding member of the Santa Clara County Black Firefighters, where he remained an active member until his retirement. He fought for justice for all people, especially people of color, and helped many social justice organizations in San Jose, surrounding communities, and Monterey, California.

Throughout their lives together, Linda and Trusty encouraged each other and their daughters to grow educationally. Trusty attended San Jose Community College and San Jose State University, while Linda continued her education until she obtained an educational doctorate. Linda often said, "Trusty seriously read so many of my books that he should have earned a doctor's degree too."

In retirement, Trusty and Linda eventually moved to Monterey, where Linda is Professor Emerita at CSUMB, and Trusty worked on his golf game. Trusty was a member of the Pacific Grove Municipal Golf Links and the Senior Men's Club.

Together, he and Linda traveled the world, spending time in France, Italy, South America, and South Africa. Trusty spoke glowingly about being in Africa just like he spoke lovingly about taking his family to meet the Bynoe family in his motherland of Barbados.

A retired Trusty was also instrumental in reuniting the retired members of the IABPFF's Southwest Region by encouraging the brothers and sisters to come together once a year for a reunion. Even in retirement, Trusty still inspired numerous people to find a career in the fire service.

When we think about it, one of the greatest traits that Dudley C. Bynoe possessed was the compassion of his heart to be a father figure to many, giving to others what he always desired for himself. Providing sound advice and encouragement to those who sought him out as an "OG" dad.

On December 25, 2022, at the age of seventy-eight, Dudley C. Bynoe was called home, and we all will forever be changed.

Dudley Bynoe is preceded in death by his parents, Dudley Samuel Bynoe and Ruby Archer Bynoe, daughter Traci Roquel Bynoe, and brother George A. Bynoe.

Dudley is survived by his wife, Dr. Linda Turner Bynoe, and daughter Nicola Desharn Bynoe, both of Monterey, California; granddaughter Ruby Rose Bynoe Holland, of Oakland, California; sister Bertha E. Bynoe Jacobs, of Syracuse, New York; brothers Winston A. Bynoe, of Greensboro, North Carolina, Terence O. Bynoe, and Myles E. Bynoe, both of New York City, New York; and many nieces and nephews.

CLINGING TO LIFE

When one is young, there is no
Thought of clinging to life
When one comes of age for love
There is no thought of clinging to life
When one starts to see the skies
Then, one starts clinging to life
When one's hair turns gray, and bones start to ache
One starts clinging to life
When one understands that life is love
Then one starts clinging to life
When one understands that there is no excuse for what he has not seen,
Then one starts clinging to life.
—"Clinging to Life," Dudley C. Bynoe (1991)

Epilogue
Trusty Bynoe

By Carl Lacey

THROUGHOUT OUR LIVES, WE meet a wide range of personalities—some are quiet and introspective, others sharp and intellectual, while some are outgoing and full of energy. But every so often, we meet someone whose personality is so expansive that it becomes a part of their very presence. Dudley "Trusty" Bynoe was one such individual. Standing tall at six foot four, with an infectious smile and a commanding presence, Trusty held strong opinions about the world, opinions he was never shy about sharing. His friends knew him as "Trusty" or simply "Bynoe," and whether you were close to him or not, he had a way of challenging you, often leaving you questioning your views while he made his known.

For more than forty years, Trusty was my closest friend and confidant. Our relationship was not one of easy agreements or placid conversations; it was built on the solid ground of mutual respect and frequent, spirited debates. We spent countless hours together, often locked in discussions that could have easily been mistaken for arguments. But we were not adversaries; we were two strong-willed men who held firm to our beliefs. Despite the sixteen-year gap between us, the respect and love we shared were deep and enduring, akin to the bond between a father and son or two brothers who always had each other's backs.

Our friendship did not have an easy beginning. We did not start as friends; in fact, we nearly came to blows the first time we met. It was a sweltering June afternoon in 1976, and I had just arrived in San Jose at the age of sixteen. That day, I joined my stepbrother Mitch Collins and his friend Greg Johnson for a basketball game against some local guys. Among them were Dudley Bynoe and Jerry Williams, two Black firefighters from the neighborhood, both in their early thirties and significantly older and stronger than us. The game was for money, and it quickly became clear that Jerry and Trusty were playing to win. Standing on the sidelines, I could not resist the urge to trash-talk, teasing these grown men for what I assumed was an attempt to take advantage of my friends.

Jerry and Trusty won the game, and Trusty, true to his nature, wasn't about to let my mouth go unchecked. He was furious and made it clear he was ready to teach me a lesson. It took months for him to let go of that first grudge, but when he finally did, it marked the beginning of a friendship that would last for more than four decades. During that time, we became closer than brothers. Sometimes, we were like father and son, other times like siblings, and occasionally, I was the father and he was the son, or vice versa. Our relationship was always contentious, but it was a good kind of contentious—one that came with a lot of laughter and mutual respect.

Trusty was a man of action, and his role as a firefighter gave him a unique flexibility with his time. We shared many days together, especially after I went off to college. His wife, Linda, worked at the phone company while pursuing her education part-time, eventually earning her doctorate in education. Together, they were a formidable team—a power couple who served as role models for many young people, myself included. When I eloped and got married, Trusty and Linda were there to witness the event, a testament to the depth of our bond.

Trusty's commitment to mentoring young Black kids was unwavering. He was a mentor under the Big Brother program in San Jose, guiding a young man named Anthony Coleman, who lived in the projects near Station 16 where Trusty worked. I got to know Anthony through Trusty, and we shared many experiences together. One year, my wife and I took a trip to Lake Tahoe with Trusty, Linda, Anthony, and his wife, Ruby. Trusty's brand of mentorship, something he called "Bynoeism," was tough love at its finest. He believed in pushing you to your limits, forcing you to stand your ground and prove your worth. For those of us who were close to him, enduring his ribbing and relentless opinions was a rite of passage. But beneath that tough exterior was a heart of gold, especially when it came to helping young Black men find their way in life.

One memorable trip to Lake Tahoe over the Christmas holidays stands out in my mind. By then, Anthony and I had enough of Trusty's relentless "Bynoeism." So, we decided to gang up on him and pummel him with snowballs. To our surprise, he took it in stride, laughing it off but not before making it clear that he would eventually get even. That was Trusty—a man who could take as well as he could give, always ready to turn a challenge into a moment of camaraderie.

Trusty's influence extended far beyond those close to him. Station 16, located on King Road in East San Jose, was in the heart of a working-class neighborhood. In the seventies, eighties, and early nineties, before the tech boom, it was common to see Trusty and his fellow firefighters standing outside the station, a group of strong, imposing Black men in uniform. For the young Black kids in the neighborhood, these men were real-life heroes long before the term "first responder" became a household phrase. They were the embodiment of possibility, role models who showed that a Black man could achieve greatness, even in a world that often tried to hold them back.

One young man, Carter French, who attended Overfelt High School, recounted a moment that changed the trajectory of his life. One day, while preparing to fry French fries, his parents called him upstairs, and in the confusion, he forgot to turn off the stove. The grease caught fire, filling the house with smoke, and the fire department had to be called. When the firefighters arrived, there was Trusty leading the charge. For Carter, seeing Trusty in uniform was a powerful moment of recognition—he saw someone who looked like him, standing tall as a firefighter, and in that instant, he knew that he could do the same. Inspired by Trusty, Carter went on to become a career firefighter.

Trusty's commitment to helping young people did not end with his retirement. He stayed actively involved in mentoring and supporting those who followed in his footsteps. Whether it was helping them navigate the challenges of joining the fire department or resolving conflicts once they were in, Trusty was always there, a steady presence that firefighters, young and old, could count on. Today, countless active and retired firefighters owe a debt of gratitude to Trusty and the Santa Clara County Black Firefighters Association for opening doors that might have otherwise remained closed.

I never became a firefighter; blood and death were not for me. I chose a different path as a businessman, and Trusty respected me for that just as I respected him for his chosen profession. But that did not mean he didn't challenge me—he did, often. Trusty's political lens was sharply focused on the inequalities of the world, and while I dealt with racism and inequality in my own field, our perspectives were different. I often admired his straightforward, in-your-face approach, wishing I could bring that same cocky sixteen-year-old attitude into the corporate world. But the reality was that paychecks and politics rarely mix well. Most of us have to choose between speaking our truth and keeping our jobs. Trusty, however, never bit his tongue. He risked it all, and though he paid a price for his outspokenness, he earned respect—even envy—from those who wished they could do the same.

Trusty was a complex man. He could be charming, intimidating, and heartfelt all at once. You either loved him or loathed him, and sometimes, you felt both emotions simultaneously. But one thing was certain: you always knew where you stood with him. Trusty kept it real, and when you were with him, he made you feel like you were the only person in the room. He used to say, "Be in the moment," and he lived his life that way—fully present, fully engaged, and always ready to take on whatever challenge came his way.

One day in college, Mitch Collins and I were spending time together with Trusty, as we often did in those days. Trusty drove a sleek black Cadillac Eldorado, a car that suited his larger-than-life personality. We had just finished lunch at a favorite Mexican restaurant when we came upon a fire that had broken out at a paint store in downtown San Jose. Although Trusty was off duty that day, he did not hesitate to respond to his duty at that moment. In a flash, he ran to the first fire truck he came upon, grabbed a random pair of turnout gear, and sprang into action like a superhero shedding his civilian clothes to don his cape. Mitch and I stuck around for a while in amazement at what we had just witnessed, but we never saw him again that day. That was Trusty—a real firefighter, always ready when duty called.

Trusty was a man who believed in being there for the people he cared about. If you needed help, he was there. If you had a problem and called him, he would show up. He was a brother you could count on, no matter what. However, Trusty was not alone in his endeavors; he had a partner in life, his wife, Linda. Together, they were a model couple, showing young Black couples what building a stable, loving family meant. Linda taught in the classroom while Trusty taught in the streets, and together, they gave a powerful example of what was possible when two people worked together toward a common goal.

One particular memory stands out: Linda invited me and my wife, Bridget, both business owners then, to speak to her students in Salinas,

California. These kids, from underserved communities in the rural farm belt, were eager to see people who looked like them, people of color who had achieved success. The gratitude on their faces is something I will never forget. Trusty and Linda showed these young people that they could achieve their dreams with hard work and determination.

Trusty and Linda were a couple that young people could admire—a beacon of stability, professionalism, and hope. They showed that you push back when the world pushes you down and never give up. Watching Linda earn her degrees, from a bachelor's to a master's and finally a doctorate, was a lesson in perseverance. Together, they led by example, opening doors for others in the corporate world, municipal government, and education.

Trust, always fond of black cars, loved to drive. In his later years, he, Linda, and his faithful companion, Assata (a purebred Shih Tzu), would travel throughout Northern and Southern California to visit sick and elderly friends and firefighters. The care and energy this couple displayed late in life, combined with empathy and compassion for others in need, was extraordinary. They were a real power couple. Linda was as active with the local Democratic party as Trusty was with the Black firefighters. As professor emeritus at Monterey Peninsula College, Linda Bynoe remains a hugely influential figure among youths from all walks of life.

Trusty and Linda Bynoe's unwavering commitment to the Black cause was what I respected most. Although the world has made strides in the past fifty years, we are not out of the woods yet. The story of Trusty Bynoe reminds us that without committed warriors like him and his ever-supportive wife, Linda, everything our ancestors fought for could be lost in a single generation. Trusty's life is a testament to the ongoing struggle for Black relevance—a love story of Blackness, family, and the fight to remain faithful to oneself in a world that often refuses to see Black people as equal.

Dudley "Trusty" Bynoe passed away on Christmas Day, December 25, 2023, standing tall even in death. He never fell to the ground, a warrior to the very end. He was my closest friend, and I will never forget him.

I spoke with the former president of the SCCBFA, Kevin Taylor, who recalled that

> those in the International Association of Black Professional Fire Fighters through the '70s, '80s, and '90s (especially the Southwest Region) knew or knew of Trusty. He was one of the Santa Clara County Black Firefighters' outspoken leaders pushing for equality and change by literally busting the doors open for my generation

to get in. Trusty was very intimidating with his 6' 5" frame, dark complexion, and that long finger you didn't want pointing at you and "giving you the business." I remember Trusty and another member from the Santa Clara County Black Firefighters Association going out of the county to Union City Fire Dept in Alameda County upon my request to aid a black firefighter being treated unfairly. They went and met with their city manager and fire chief and explained things with that finger in their faces, and let's just say that things worked out for the black firefighter.

As President of the SCCBFA, I had to go in front of the media. In one particular case against Gremminger, a firefighter who shot a young black kid in The Great Mall parking lot playing vigilante justice, Trusty stood behind me like a warrior keeping watch. He also had my and others' backs on many occasions if we were in trouble. Bynoe would come through if we were in need but would chew you a new one if necessary, and in my opinion, he was just a REAL GOOD Man/Brother.

Bynoe and his wife Linda are like Big Brother and Big Sister to Lenora and me, and I loved those positive, uplifting, motivational conversations he'd have with me and many of my brothers. Whether it was about life, marriage, fire Service, golf, etc, he was gonna make you feel better about whatever it was. He loved his family, friends, golf, and his Shih Tzu. After he retired in the mid/late 90s, he certainly softened up some because he was no longer in the "fight." He smiled more, laughed more, but could still talk shit with the best of em: a strong brother, father, husband, mentor, fighter who loved you strong.

You will be missed, Big Brother Trust. We love you, RIP, and don't raise too much ruckus in Heaven.[1]

---

1. Kevin Taylor, in a private message to Carl Lacey.

Bibliography

Bay Area Census. "City of San Jose: Santa Clara County." California Bureau of Labor Statistics. https://sj-admin.s3-us-west-2.amazonaws.com/0000_0000_ BayAreaCensus_CityofSJSCCounty.pdf.

Bogle, Donald. *Toms, Coons, Mulattoes, Mammies, and Bucks: An Interpretive History of Blacks in American Films*. New York: Bloomsbury, 2001.

Charles River Editors. *Black Wall Street and the Tulsa Race Massacre*. Las Vegas, NV: Charles River Editors, 2025.

Chen, Sandie Angulo. "What Was Life Like in NYC in the Roaring Twenties?" Ancestry, May 21, 2021. https://www.ancestry.com/c/ancestry-blog/what-was-life-like-in-nyc-in-the-roaring-twenties.

Finz, Stacy. "Ex-Fireman Sentenced to 9 Years for Mall Slaying / Wife of Victim Asked for Longer Sentence." SFGate, Feb. 7, 1998. https://www.sfgate.com/news/article/ex-fireman-sentenced-to-9-years-for-mall-slaying-3013180.php.

Forde, F. Donnie. *Caribbean Americans in New York City 1895–1975*. Images of America. Charleston, SC: Arcadia, 2002.

Gonzales, Sandra. "Gremminger Bail Request Denied." *Mercury News* (CA), Feb. 18, 1998.

Gray, Tom. "Union Funds Taken, Firefighters Put Official on Leave." *Mercury News* (CA), Nov. 16, 1990.

Greenlee, Sam. *The Spook Who Sat by the Door*. Detroit: Wayne State University Press, 1969.

Hampton, Millard. "The African American Firefighters Crisis: They Won the Court Case and Have Redeemed Their Reputation of Excellence in Santa Clara Valley; Dudley 'Trusty' Bynoe Tells His Version to the African-Descent Community." *Exodus*, Feb. 1996.

Henry, Patrick. "Jackie Robinson: Athlete and American Par." *Virginia Quarterly Review* 73 (1997) 189–203. https://www.jstor.org/stable/26439091.

Inda, Estella. "East Side Revelations—The Ribbs." San Jose Public Library, Feb. 9, 2022. https://www.sjpl.org/blogs/post/east-side-revelations-the-ribbs/.

James, Joy, ed. *The Angela Y. Davis Reader*. Maldon, MA: Blackwell, 1998.

Kyckelhahn, Tracey, and Thomas H. Cohen. "Civil Rights Complaints in U.S. District Courts, 1990–2006." NCJ 222989. Washington, DC: Bureau of Justice Statistics, Aug. 2008. https://bjs.ojp.gov/content/pub/pdf/crcusdco6.pdf.

Library of Congress. "The Murder of Emmett Till." *Jet Magazine*, 1955. https://www.loc.gov/collections/civil-rights-history-project/articles-and-essays/murder-of-emmett-till/.

Michaeli, Ethan. *The Defender: How the Legendary Black Newspaper Changed America*. New York: Mariner, 2018.

Milton, Nerissa L. "The Dorie Miller Trophy Award." *Negro History Bulletin* 19.4 (1956) 93. http://www.jstor.org/stable/44212952.

Mowatt, Raoul V. "Retrial Opens in Bias Lawsuit Firefighters: Ex-City Manager Had Papers in Office Kitchen Relating to Case." *Mercury News* (CA), May 7, 1999.

Romano, Bill. "Fire Chief Gets Credit." *Mercury News* (CA), Aug. 14, 1998.

Schick, Joshua. "USS *Mason*: First in Its Class." National WWII Museum, Feb. 12, 2021. https://www.nationalww2museum.org/war/articles/uss-mason-us-navy.

Singh, Gary. "Exploring the Cultural Geography of San Jose's East Side." *Metro Silicon Valley*, Jan. 17, 2018. https://www.metrosiliconvalley.com/exploring-the-cultural-geography-of-san-joses-east-side/.

Westcott, Diane Nilsen. "Blacks in the 1970's: Did They Scale the Job Ladder?" *Monthly Labor Review* 6 (1982) 29–38. https://www.bls.gov/opub/mlr/1982/06/art5full.pdf.

Wikipedia. "International Association of Black Professional Firefighters." Wikimedia Foundation, last modified Mar. 21, 2025. https://en.wikipedia.org/wiki/International_Association_of_Black_Professional_Firefighters.

———. "Joe Louis." Wikimedia Foundation, last modified Mar. 11, 2025. https://en.wikipedia.org/wiki/Joe_Louis.

Wilson, Carol Ann. *Still Point of the Turning World: The Life of Gia-fu Feng*. Portland, OR: Amber Lotus, 2009.

Witt, Barry. "Firefighter's Discipline Largely Upheld Panel Decides City Proved Most Charges." *Mercury News* (CA), Sept. 6, 1997.

———. "Trial of Fire Chief Begins Suit: Says Old Guard of Whites Sought to Deny Blacks Promotions." *Mercury News* (CA), July 29, 1998.

www.ingramcontent.com/pod-product-compliance
Lightning Source LLC
Chambersburg PA
CBHW072237270326
41930CB00010B/2167